DRAWN IN

TROY BRONSINK

DRAWN IN

A CREATIVE PROCESS FOR ARTISTS,
ACTIVISTS, AND JESUS FOLLOWERS

PARACLETE PRESS
BREWSTER, MASSACHUSETTS

2013   First Printing

Drawn In: A Creative Process for Artists, Activists, and Jesus Followers

Copyright © 2013 by Ink Born Story, Inc.

ISBN 978-1-55725-871-7

Library of Congress Cataloging-in-Publication Data

Bronsink, Troy.
   Drawn in : a creative process for artists, activists, and Jesus followers /
   Troy Bronsink.
      p. cm.
   Includes bibliographical references and index.
   ISBN 978-1-55725-871-7 (trade pbk.)
1. Artists—Religious life. 2. Creative ability—Religious aspects—
Christianity. 3. Creation (Literary, artistic, etc.)—Religious aspects-
   BV4596.A78B76 2012
   248.8'8—dc23   2012030780

10 9 8 7 6 5 4 3 2 1

Published by Paraclete Press
Brewster, Massachusetts
www.paracletepress.com
Printed in the United States of America

contents

Beauty bids all things come
    to itself (and thus
        we call it beauty).
Just so, it gathers
    all things trembling
        fully to itself.

—PSUEDO-DIONYSIOS
(FIFTH-CENTURY CHRISTIAN TEACHER)[1]

There is a cultural change afoot, and it's exciting.

For some, this change brings with it a welcome shift in priorities, as we've moved from a society of Agrarian-Age farm workers to Industrial-Age factory workers to the Information-Age knowledge workers we are, now, transitioning again to a society of Inventive-Age creatives.

With these changes we have seen a shift not only in the tools we use but also in the way people think, and in the values and aesthetics people prefer. In other words, from head to heart to stomach to hands we find ourselves in a new world.

While the Industrial and Information Ages gave great credence to order and predictability and valued what could be counted (features that are often seen as left-brain ways of thinking), this new age finds valuable creators, meaning makers, and activist listeners.

The church of this age will value right-brain ways of functioning. There are many reasons for these shifts, but regardless of their origins, these new cultural norms are here to stay.

It is in this context that Troy Bronsink invites us into the story of God and creation. *Drawn In* is set squarely in the sensibility of creativity and the meaning-making age. Many of us, including me, do not define ourselves as artists: we can't draw or paint, sing or shape clay. And for too long, being an artist was reserved for the elites in certain disciplines. But as *Drawn In* reminds us, we're more than artists in the classic sense: we are given creative gifts by the Creator.

Not only are we wonderfully made, but also we're made to wonder. We are a people who not only tell the story of God but also are called by God to be creative people. God creates and so do we.

What makes this new age exciting for so many is that it opens an invitation to part of the story of God that has been too long reserved for only a select few. We see the acts of Dreaming, Hovering, Risking, Listening, Generating, and Resting are not only what God does but also what we have been created to do.

This call is for the individual, but it is also for communities. While each of us will play our individual role, we must create the communities, the structures, and the living, collective experiences where these realities blossom.

This opens the door to Jesus' call to his disciples: do even greater things than I have done (Jn. 14:12). This expands the challenge to "fill the earth and subdue it" (Gen. 1:28). This roots the promise of Jesus that his community will receive power when the Holy Spirit comes to "be my witnesses in Jerusalem, and in all Judea and Samaria, and to the ends of the earth" (Acts 1:8). This echoes the daring witness of the early followers of the Way: "To him who is able to do immeasurably more than all we ask or imagine, according to his power that is at work within us, to him be glory in the church and in Christ Jesus throughout all generations, for ever and ever! Amen" (Eph. 3:20–21).

On a cool Georgia September evening, fifty people with wine glasses, berets, old T-shirts, rich and poor, educated and uneducated sat outside the shed of my neighbor Dorothy O'Conner. The bonfire was burning forty yards away in her courtyard, but we were all in her narrow driveway, staring. I sat, legs crossed, next to my seven-year-old daughter, who had her sketchpad in hand. Our friend Daley was crowded in behind us with his whizbang professional digital camera. We were all stunned, grinning ear to ear.

In front of us all was a surreal still life of a woman lost at sea. Half of the hewn stern of her small boat stuck out toward us. In it a live model wearing a nineteenth-century dress sat knitting a black blanket and looking, really pining, out the window. The floor of Dorothy's shed was wide weathered clapboard. Over it poured an ocean made of moss, colored knit afghan blankets, seashells, and skeletons of all sorts of crustaceans: horseshoe crabs, blue crabs, lobsters. From the roof hung hundreds of strands of Spanish moss. The three walls opening to us were like the inside of an old ship covered with netting, tobacco pipes, oil paintings of the sea in gilded frames, and oval silver-tin mirrors. It all fit into a simple 1920s two-car garage, but it felt like a window into Terabithia or Narnia.

Dorothy, a photographer who has received national acclaim for her installations, revives the classic form of *tableau vivant*: costumed actors placed in an ornate setting as a form of still life. But instead of keeping her acclaimed staging arrangement exclusive for her own photographs, Dorothy shares these arrangements with other great Atlanta photographers, as well as amateurs like me, children like my daughter, and even our poorer neighbors in Southwest Atlanta—everyone was free to take it all in. All who would come were invited into her art. It is an enormous feat of generosity for a starving artist. Dorothy has thrown at least six parties like this with different sets and models, giving away months of work for free every time.

In all my time involved with church and ministry, as a singer-songwriter, consultant, pastor, or fan of public art, Dorothy's gift with beauty and invitation stands in a league of its own. The same way she crafts photographs from negatives, silvers, and emulsions, Dorothy sets out to curate a beautiful space that can be shared. Her art is much more than something to observe, it is a happening. Her art is a free gift, drawing us in.

The art of God is similarly free to be enjoyed by all. God's art is not secret or exclusive. It is not vain or self-serving. God doesn't use beauty to sneak in an undesirable ingredient. The beauty of this world is a free gift of God and part-and-parcel of what God is already up to. In fact, God draws us more deeply into the very creation of which we are already necessarily a part. Like a director inspiring actors on the set, the Creator continually breathes life into you and me. God, in fact, breathes life into every part of the material world, and will do so like an everlasting well, drawing all things into one grand vision of creation. We, artists, all of us, are part of this beautiful creative-divine process.

The purpose of this book is to sketch out these correlations between the *creative life* and the *life of faith* by tracing how God creatively draws all things into one vision of a new creation. Whether you are a teacher, a parent, or a barista, your craft is the very locus of God's artistic vision come to life. When you pray, "Your will be done on earth as it is in heaven," God answers with your everyday life. And those of us involved in the art of church are no different, in this sense, than the professional studio drummer or the water colorist. Our faith comes to life when it pours from our calling, and our calling blooms when we apply craft and intention to our actions. There is a way that Life draws you and me in deeper. In that unforced creative place the beautiful colors, flavors, and processes are meant to be enjoyed!

Why is it, then, that so many artists throughout Western history have had an ambivalent or combative relationship with those committed to the art of church? I don't mean simple critiques of church artists or so-called "sacred arts," but a philosophical difference between the artist's prophetic craft and the craft of developing and maintaining church. Marshall McLuhan coined the famous phrase "the method is the message." And artists are frequently the first to line up to point out that church methods don't match our message.

Vincent van Gogh, the painter, a son of a preacher, found the joy of painting after a three-year failed earnest venture in church and mission among the poor. Michelangelo and Leonardo da Vinci forever danced between the service of the church commissions and their own religious discovery. Andy Warhol would paint ironic portrayals of the Last Supper, and yet it was discovered posthumously that he had secretly attended Catholic Mass at Saint Vincent Ferrer throughout his life. The fictional character of Chaim Potok's *My Name Is Asher Lev* depicts this tension between arts and religion when he attempts to justify to his Hasidic father why he must defy Jewish prohibitions and continue painting nudes.

> "I'm part of a tradition, Papa. Mastery of the art form of the nude is very important to that tradition. Every artist who ever lived drew or painted the nude. . . . I don't want to sit in a room painting for myself. I want to communicate what I do. And I want critics to know I can do it. . . . I respect you, Papa. But I can't respect your aesthetic blindness."[2]

While the arts are frequently antagonistically positioned against religion in general, and this often happens specifically within Christianity, most creatives are compelled by the very love that Christian churches testify to. A loving partnership with the Creator need not blind us aesthetically, neither does artistic passion blind a person to faith. Author Madeleine L'Engle describes this as "a listening, unself-conscious love," and she writes that "many artists who are incapable of this in their daily living are able to find it as they listen to their work, that work which binds our wounds and heals us and helps us toward wholeness."[3] Somehow the partnership between beauty and God's transformational love does not escape the eye of the artist.

I like the way one of my teachers has put it, "The what and how of God's mission, as it unfolds, is always congruent to the why of God's love . . . [which God's] story reveals."[4] Darrell Guder wrote this after years spent comparing contemporary Western culture's relationship with the church to that of non-Western culture's relationship with missionary churches. This course of study (called missiology) points to the blind spots and the unappreciated ways that the gospel shows up within and beyond the walls of organized religion. Artists like Michelangelo, van Gogh, and Warhol had to leave the aesthetic blindness of church to follow the "listening unself-conscious love" of their callings, and this may have been the case for you, too. My own meanderings between expressions of Christianity and public art have been marked by this conflict. The stories and metaphors I'll share come from my own process in integrating that artistic love with the Christian story of God's love.

This book is designed to intentionally widen or deepen your creative life and faith. For fifteen years, in conferences, galleries, living rooms, and churches across the United States, I've been working with artistic people of faith and church leaders to emphasize how *church is an art*, a subset of disciplines intended to be applied to the stuff of life. This book aims to deepen and connect both the creative life (of all of us) and the unfolding life of the missional church.

Where This Book Began

I started this book a few years ago because of several encounters I had with varied creative people of Christian faith.

The first conversation was over dinner with a few young artist friends, Anders and Jenni.[5] We had become friends years earlier when we met at a conference in New Mexico at similar life stages, leaving the churches we had been raised in. Since then many from that group have dropped by while passing through Atlanta. Anders and Jenni did so one summer between photo shoots, studio gigs, church shows, and band bar tours. Their short visits to our slower urban environment were like a retreat for them and an adventure for us. We shared favorite songs, made dinners from scratch, and stayed up late drinking, sharing favorite chocolates, and smoking. We would take walks around my inner-city neighborhood and they would help put our daughter to bed. They had been on the road for three months straight and, like a lot of touring musicians, one of them had developed a dependency on alcohol to quiet the rational self and get into the music night after night. They were spent, but they didn't know how to slow down.

Church didn't allow them to slow down (when they went it was just one more gig) nor did church inspire them to create (they were simply filling a slot). They knew there was a quieter place that their creativity could pour out of, but they were too concerned about making headway to dare to stop the perpetual motion. Like so many others, artists or not, in the modern compulsive life of stimulant after stimulant, they were regulating output demands with instant Tweets, news feeds, espresso to get up, and alcohol to mellow down.

That same week I had a conversation with my brother, Jonathan, a graphic designer who was pushing himself as a small business owner while also directing a marketing department of a small university. To make ends meet he was juggling his job with side projects for political candidates. He had tried to attend a small-town Bible church for a while, but eventually their conversations and teaching, and rules for membership, didn't make much sense to him. His experience of religious community felt disingenuous, like his contract work for political marketers that he used to pay his bills. He wanted to follow his muse, he wanted to follow his life dreams with his wife, he wanted to pay his bills, but he also wanted to integrate all of this with his Christian faith. And so for that season in his life, Jonathan remained an artist with his two feet in the separate worlds of passionate creativity and passionless work for "the man." His faith had to wait on the shelf as an external category to check in on periodically. I have found that many artists and activists live like my brother did—closeted about their faith because there don't seem to be words or communities expressing faith in a way that can catch up to their real-life experience.

There is a third type of creative person who inspired this book. The same month that Anders and Jenni stopped by, I attended a conference for church artists and pastors set in the hill country of Texas. Unlike my brother, most of the folks there were "all in" with their congregations. Many were fortunate enough to find a livelihood or sustainable part-time gig in various arts as an actor, designer, or band member, yet these folks struggled to be that same creative self in their faith communities. Unfortunately, some of these talented folks only get called upon to lead in their faith communities in order to serve as that proverbial spoon full of sugar to help a congregation swallow the supposed "real content," or as last-minute window dressing for a predetermined thesis. The design of spaces, bulletins, projection, materials, song arrangements, even some churches that use dance or children's performances—all of these are sequestered to the "arts" serving to support the "interpretive" and "formational" work of worship. So even though these artists have unique capacities to see, explore, or create in ways that could be transformative in their communities, they often end up reshuffling standards from contemporary Christian praise and worship music or get sent a finalized sermon series with instructions to make the website or handouts more attractive to a certain market sector.

Sequestering artists to changing the window dressing of a church often leaves them feeling more alone than ever. These artists have to live a sort of double life. Their creative self thrives as a sort of alter ego to their churchy self. They don't quite recognize their creative calling within the Bible or the denominational tradition they contribute to, but they want to. Some artists in this situation even use religion to regulate their compulsions; for them, faith operates more like their creative engine's governor than its spark or fuel. And so, even these church artists tend to feel disintegrated, secretly looking for free places to really get creative. Gregory Wolfe writes about this disintegration:

> Too many efforts to relate religion and the arts have stumbled because they attempt to channel the imagination into pious patterns. At the root of this failure is an underlying fear of the imagination itself—a force that can't be tamed or made to fit into comforting, predictable categories. . . . But art in its highest pitch tries to tell us things we don't know, or have forgotten, and that can be unsettling.[6]

Maybe you recognize yourself or someone close to you in one of the three examples of my friends. Whether you're the manically self-destructive creative, the closeted spiritual person, or the resigned double-life creative, I believe you can find creative inspiration and productivity when you are drawn into something larger, when you can live as part of a larger grand creative work of God. I wanted to write this book for all of these friends of mine, reintroducing them to the inspiration and sustenance of God's creative love within that "highest pitch" that Greg Wolfe talks about.

So I set out, but I didn't get clear about why I *felt drawn to write* in this season of my life until some of my own life began running up against walls, when some of my own dreams were falling apart, and new responsibilities and circumstances came along challenging the ways I had once felt alive.

I became aware of my own desire to tame my life and forget those things that frightened me the most. I realized that I too had compulsions I was using to get out of my head. I realized that even though I was a pastor with a lot of freedom to determine the direction of the faith community in which I belonged, I too was still captive to my fears and ambitions. I realized that I too was compromising creativity in order to belong. I realized that I too long for deeper integration.

To address this "fear of imagination" head on, I needed language that could reintroduce art and faith. To be clear, I don't think this is an "alternative" approach for "alternative" artsy submarkets, or a be-all-end-all paradigm for creativity or mission. This is intended to be synthesis, complimentary, and freeing. I've synthesized several emerging insights that seem to resonate with one another, and I believe this book's contents can coexist in a complimentary way with many paradigms (theologies or work environments) in which you may already be operating. But I do think it may offer some freedom from gridlocks or creative blocks you are running up against in your own life, craft, family, church, or business.

Drawn In is designed to walk you past ambition into rhythms of inspiration, creation, and rest. It is designed to offer integrative language for collaboration between artist and faith leaders. You'll match images with your own personal reflection to combine the work of life with the visions of beauty and God's work in the world. Along the way you'll get to know stories and practices of other artists, activists, and Jesus followers.

In the course of writing this book, I worked closely on the formation and subsequent closing of an emergent church plant, the explosive growth of another where I led music and produced an album, the founding and succession-plan of a community nonprofit, the "surprise" of a newborn son, and record-breaking economic shifts shared with my urban neighbors and the rest of the world in this early twenty-first century. Among these and other "stress-chart busters" I realized that I had grown increasingly driven instead of drawn. It turns out, two years after having proposed the title, *Drawn In*, those words really explain it best.

This book is designed to be a retreat, an exit ramp away from what Emmylou Harris so poignantly described as "earning [our] stumble into grace" and an onramp toward what Jesus described as "learn[ing] the unforced rhythms of grace."[7]

Like any work of art, the reward of working through a book like this is given to those that donate part of themselves to the effort. As in yoga or piano playing, practice is the real arena for growth. Likewise, the depth of saturation of the metaphors and constructs in this book will depend upon the depth of your participation. Through these pages I'm offering exercises and readings designed to gradually draw you into a bigger, freer, regenerative story.

How to Use This Book

Here at the beginning, I suggest you find a fresh, unique journal or sketchbook to hold your reflections and take a look at your average weekly schedule and make a few regular appointments to work through the exercises.

The book is set out in two parts: God's creative work, and then ours. In section 1, "God's Relationship with Creation" we'll explore the *rhythms of creativity*, a six-wave cycle integrating Scripture and tradition with emerging creative systems theory.

Then we'll walk through the ingredients of creativity:- *time*, *space*, and *matter*. Last, we'll explore the *collaborative* nature of God's work.

In section two, "Our Relationship with Creation," we'll begin with *incarnation*, an ancient Christian teaching about the integration of the divine with material world. We'll then see the ramifications of incarnation on the artist's own job to integrate *vision* and *work*. Finally, we'll conclude by retracing the six waves of God's creative work as *our own rhythms*—as "God's handiwork, created in Christ Jesus to do good works, which God prepared in advance for us to do" (Ephesians 2:10 NIV).

I'll invite you at various points to stop or to go on a walk, to draw things, to sit in contemplation, to sing, to read, or to journal. Rest assured, these are only suggestions—no religious or artistic training is required. For those turned off by the vocabulary and postures of Christianity, I have worked to translate my words into terms shared across many faith backgrounds. For those terrified to draw or to whistle a tune, simple markings on paper or playing music on an iPod will do. Much in the way that a child is unintimidated by the crayon on the floor, you're invited to gently live into what Catholic priest, Thomas Merton, echoing the Zen of Shunryu Suzuki, has called "beginner's mind":

> One cannot begin to face the real difficulties of the life of prayer and meditation unless one is first perfectly content to be a beginner and really experience himself as one who knows little or nothing, and has a desperate need to learn the bare rudiments. Those who think they "know" from the beginning will never, in fact, come to know anything.[8]

You may want to find a friend or two with whom you can work through *Drawn In*, sharing the exercises with one another at points along the way. If you are a church leader or parent looking to be more deeply acquainted with your own creative impulses, consider inviting a few creatives nearby to be a guide for you in the process—you'll be surprised to discover how much they will appreciate seeing this through your eyes as well.

A Further Note about Who This Book Is For

Drawn In is not explicitly for worship leaders or activists— it is for every person who wants to follow Jesus and do it through their creativity. That said, I'm convinced that there is a significant resonance for readers of these two fields, and would like to make a nod toward that before we really dig in.

The idea of creativity is more commonplace these days beyond even the starving artists of Greenwich Village or the highfalutin' halls of the Louvre or the Julliard School. Many today identify with creativity because we live in an age of popular design consciousness where kids watch fashion designers on *Project Runway*, and busy parents can order handmade crafts online at Etsy.com or internationally crafted goods at Ten Thousand Villages. These days in Atlanta, you can walk around local parks and see public art flash mobs or drive past guerilla art posters on alley walls the likes of Banksy and Shepard Fairey. Technophiles download TED (Technology, Entertainment, and Design) podcasts or order apps for handheld devices to create their own sound tracks and organize their daily habits. Everywhere we turn there are new stores or campaigns that bring people into "Art" or participation. And this is just as prolific in the church professional world. I work with congregations all over who are starting "arts ministries" to do everything from discipleship with artists, to curating participatory worship installations, to adding visual design elements to print, web, and projected communications.

Ellen and Julie Lupton are sisters who are graphic and literary designers. They write in their book, *D.I.Y.: Design It Yourself*, that culture has "arrived at a compelling turn in the evolution of design consciousness. The general public is more aware than ever of the values of language and design, from graphics to architecture to automobiles. At the same time, many consumers . . . distrust the global corporate economy upon which mass production relies."[9] They suggest that this transition has allowed for a reemergence of new "organic intellectuals" who can "merge physical and mental labor, building 'new modes of thought' out of acts of doing and making."[10] Do-It-Yourselfers have less to lose than others once had in experimenting and adjusting to the limits of their own context. In the process, they have more to discover as well. This DIY revolution reminds me of the integrative language of John's Gospel: "No one has ever seen God; if we love one another, God lives in us, and his love is perfected in us" (1 John 4:12 NRSV).

So I take as my challenge—in life, as well as in this book—something similar; that is, to organically make connections between the creative God and the creative self by doing work with the everyday elements of creative life: vision, work, and materials. My hunch is that these three elements are also essential parts to the creative life with God. In fact, God's own creative drawing-in is an integration of vision, work, and material.

Art draws on our vision—that intangible place of calling, imagination, intuition, and taste. Vision and work meet "where the rubber hits the road," transforming certain material things into something else. Or as one of my friend's T-shirts reads, "I Make Stuff Up." In life as in art, our selection of materials, and the choice to use one ingredient over another, can make all the difference.

As such, worship styles are also choices made by artists to aesthetically engage participants with a particular vision. This is not a book about worship curation or a vision for the church and the arts.[11] It is important, however, to note how often we find ourselves in church leadership circles caught in cul-de-sacs debating worship styles because we see the importance of marrying vision with the essential materials of human life. In this case, worship styles are just like other intentional creative decisions—they are strategies for integrating vision and work. I hopé the language and exercises of this book will help open new thoroughfares beyond those cul-de-sacs.

In a similar way, activism involves deliberate choices about practices and selectiveness concerning materials. Whether you're paying an extra fifty cents for fair trade chocolates, taking the time to rinse out your cans to recycle, shopping at a local farmer's market, buying Tom's shoes, or staging a public antigreed demonstration, you are making strategic decisions about how your life will be fashioned, organized, or staged. Today, leaders ranging from intentional Christian communities to social entrepreneurs are speaking of intentional choices that take seriously things like location, purchase power, and collaboration. And yet, from my own experiences in urban nonprofit work, many of these groups are captive to a disintegrated drivenness that betrays their very vision of an abundant, lovely, and equitable society. It is my hope that readers from these backgrounds will also find renewed freedom and energy as they are drawn into a love broader than any of their singular creative commitments and callings.

Don't Miss the *Glory* for the Trees

One final point of introduction: like most artists (and pastors—I'm one of those too), I want you to like me. The act of writing a book on spiritual formation can be like putting a picture of me with God on my Facebook page hoping you'd see it and "like" me. So I hope that the crutches I'm leaving behind don't clutter up the pathway. My scars and fears, and even my gifts, are just that: mine. So please, when these are conspicuous, see past my delivery and seek between the lines how the breath of God might draw you in, and how you might draw in God as well. Take the images and practices and freely try them on until they are your own. Share them. But if you find them to serve lifeless ends such as compulsivity or escapism, drop them like bad religion and return to God who is drawing all things to God's self.

The Hebrew prophet Ezekiel, a bit of a tortured artist himself, envisioned God's glory as a huge burning wheel, always on the move, unable to be channeled or contained, at once approaching and departing. My hope is that this book opens our senses to God in a similarly evocative yet hard-to-domesticate way.

GOD'S RELATIONSHIP WITH CREATION

Our Creator and the "Lost Arts" of Creativity

Most art goes from start to finish in unconventional ways. You can almost watch beauty emerge whenever time is spent marrying the material world with skill and ingenuity. Whether you're watching a musician, a dancer, a poet, or a painter create, you will frequently notice a glimmer in the artist's eye associated with surprise, wonder, curiosity, and play.

Perhaps God's "eyes" glimmer while creating as well.

If we, who are made in the image of God, are to understand our relationship to the world around us, we would do well to understand the Creator's relationship with us. The Hebrew poet wrote, "Taste and see that the LORD is good" (Psalm 34:8 NIV). Rediscovering God's creator relationship to us, and all the beauty we taste and see, can reintroduce us to our own creative callings.

God's creativity woos us into experiencing how love functions. God's creativity, as portrayed in Scripture and history, can inform and compliment how we view the mission of God and God's people in this day and age. God is like an engineer with the world's greatest imagination. Let's call God, then, the *imagineer*. Studying the creative process of God's imagineering from the first chapter of Genesis and elsewhere in Scripture, we might rediscover God's "lost arts" of creativity.

Irish poet and philosopher John O'Donohue liked to say that everyone is an artist: we are all "ex-kids" who once had great imaginations, and we all fashion parts of our lived environments. If we go back to the very beginning we see that God, too, puts imagination to work. You may already feel comfortable with the idea of God making, creating, fashioning. But have you ever wondered what God's creativity looked like before "the beginning" or since? And when the apostle Paul and others after him plumbed the depths of the significance of Christ's resurrection with the language of "new creation" what more could we learn about God's creative rhythms?

Many of our assumptions about God separate creation from everyday work, as if the greatest leaps in imagination or greatest risks of love have already been taken, and we're simply left to recreate great moments. Exploring the creative ways of God, in whose image we are created, can instruct our current practices in the New Creation before us.

It's a stretch to determine if God was somewhere before the origins of time and matter, but it's clear that something was going on before the big beginning. If you read the thousands of stories told in Scripture, and the other testimonies that faith communities would exchange through oral tradition and hand-delivered scrolls across the Middle East, North Africa, and Europe and eventually to you, you see gestures toward what was going on before the first verse of Genesis when "God created." It appears that God was not frozen in timelessness waiting to thaw out. And God was not alone in meditation with some "strong inner world" like a socially awkward savant. Rather, God has preexisted as an interrelated community, as persons whom the Scriptures often introduce as the Father, the Son, and the Holy Spirit, in a dance of mutual submission, one serving the other.

This is important because the Creating God in our story has never existed as a lonely note, but more like a chord, a harmony of distinct notes setting off each other with interrelated ringing.[12] This interrelationship is what the Christian tradition would later call the Trinity and define with terms such as "separate but not confused." The practice of the Original Artist, then, from the very beginning, was one of free self-giving other-relatedness.[13]

Vincent van Gogh wrote that "Christ . . . is more of an artist than the artists; he works in the living spirit and the living flesh; he makes *men* instead of statues."[14] For years, working with pastors and artists I began to wonder, how does God's everyday "making of humans" relate to our own everyday creative work? A great deal of research and innovation about creative process has emerged in the last two decades. Various processes have been laid out ranging from those of Stanford's d.school, the global "human-centered" design firm IDEO, Julia Cameron's *Artist's Way*, as well as popular psychology best sellers such as Mihaly Csikszentmihalyi's *Flow* and *Creativity*. Such works point to the fact that art cannot be fully appreciated as a final product but that the way of the artist and the creative process is itself an art.

In this chapter I'll propose a cycle, with six waves, to explore how we might learn from God's own design process or creative way. Those six waves are: *dreaming > hovering > risking > listening > reintegrating > resting*, and they operate at large and small scales, cyclically from beginning to ending to beginning again.

Noticing Artists exercise 1

Have you ever considered God to be artist? Write down the names of some artists you know in person. In what ways are their lives examples of God's own creative capacities? If you don't know any, find an art gallery, theater, studio, or small music venue nearby and visit it this week. Notice the artist's statement, the testimony of the work and desires of the artist. Notice the relationship between the artist and his or her dreams, materials, and contexts. Do you see connections to the way God relates to you and me and this world in which we live? Take twenty minutes or so to journal on what you've noticed.

Next, look in the book of Job at chapters 38 and 39. Poets from the wisdom tradition have a special way of bringing beauty in as a form of persuasion. Job has endured unbelievable loss, only made worse by the unsolicited advice of three peers and his own wife. Eventually Job has had enough and enters into an argument with God—to which God responds. The response is God's own poetic artist's statement about the work of creation. "Where were you when I laid the earth's foundation?" God asks (Job 38:4 NIV). What do you notice about the Creator's dreams and delights from this statement?

(Wave 1 of 6)

God's *dreams* love the future into existence

God's creativity began with a dream. The textile artist has a deep hunch about what colors or what textures the weaving must include. Before picking up a guitar, the musician can seem almost obsessed with an unshakable idea. The singer-songwriter intuits what story has to be told through her song. The visionary sees the pieces of the puzzle and is working to make them fit just right.

Much has been explored in modern creative theory about the connections between design and vision.[15] The imagineer is someone who combines vision, long-range thinking, and playful experimentation.

Walt Disney is the one who first popularized the term *Imagineer*, to describe artists, engineers, and designers who bring environments to life in Disney motion pictures and theme parks. But imagineering was reportedly first used by engineers and aluminum workers in World War II to describe "the fine art of deciding where we go from here." It is the implementation of creative ideas into practical forms.

When we think of our origins, we often read the accounts in Genesis, Job, and elsewhere as a report of the recipe, in exclusion of the dreams behind them. We will talk about the ingredients of God's great art project in a future chapter, but before we get ahead of ourselves let's look at the *way* and possibly scratch at the *why* of that creative process.

If you were to walk through an amusement park ride or a mall or an art gallery with a friend who is an engineer, designer, or architect, it would not be long before they would get you thinking about "why" the artifact was built. "What were they thinking?" we'd ask. An imagineer recognizes the cooperation between what we're thinking and what we're doing. An imagineer mashes up the "dreaming" with the "making."

Buckminster "Bucky" Fuller was a designer/architect most known for his geodesic domes, such as the huge silver golf ball–shaped home of Spaceship Earth in Disney World's Epcot Center. In the modern age of design he popularized a form of reverse engineering called "design science." Applying to design what he observed scientists doing in their scientific process, he found a way to prioritize dreaming above utility or linear problem solving.

In Fuller's time, an engineer would get hired by a developer and architect wanting to build a bridge between one thing and another. Such an engineer would not typically be a part of the decision, asking "why." The result was that things were being built in modern cities and homes with little to no coordination to the needs of the end user, and little connection to the shared built environment. In response, Fuller revolutionized design by beginning with the concept that things belong to *one whole*. Fuller would invent technologies in order to change people's options. Fuller and his futurists would dream of what they wanted to see happen and then would work backwards as a team of experts to get the project to a place where it could happen.

In fact, many of Fuller's domes were not even possible when he first designed them. They had to wait for the technology to catch up to the vision. But that didn't stop Fuller from designing an environment where such buildings would be possible once everything came together. He writes:

> The function of what I call *design science* is to solve problems by introducing into the environment new artifacts, the availability of which will induce their spontaneous employment by humans and thus, coincidentally, cause humans to abandon their previous problem-producing behaviors and devices. For example, when humans have a vital need to cross the roaring rapids of a river, as a design scientist I would design them a bridge, causing them, I am sure, to abandon spontaneously and forever the risking of their lives by trying to swim to the other shore.[16]

What if our Creator is also this sort of imagineer or design scientist? Jesus taught his followers to pray that God would "lead us not into temptation" but "deliver us from evil." What would it mean for our worship and church forming practices to see God as an artistic visionary, working with the created world by placing artifacts in this emerging world to accomplish this prayer? What if *you and I* are some of those artifacts? And if so, what is involved in God's process of creating such artifacts? These are some of the questions addressed in the upcoming chapters.

There is a lot of talk in Christian leadership circles today about the *missional church* rooted in the mission of God. The missional shift is from success-driven models of church toward relational models, demonstrating Jesus' self-sacrificing love and seeking justice in the wider world. But what difference would it make if we began to not only follow God's mission but also God's way of accomplishing that mission, God's creative "imagineering" character? What if God was not just the ultimate visionary, but also the ultimate risk taker, a generous self-sacrificing kind of creator who would let go of "equality in the heavenly realm" to serve the whole? Might we have something to learn from that kind of God, too? If so, it is possible that we have forgotten God's arts.

In the book *Cradle to Cradle*, chemist-designers William McDonough and Michael Braungart describe an emerging approach to design that asks about the full life cycle of a product from production, to use, to disposal, to disintegration. Life cycle designers seek to create things that benefit the world at each stage. And so they design everything from waterproof books that will be completely recyclable to buildings that can be repurposed, from city plans that account for generational growth or decline to plant-based plastic flatware that can be composted. They design with a long view.

God is an imagineer with such a long view.

Imagine with me: there the triune God was, before the beginning, abiding in love and imagineering with the long view. Together, sharing love and dreaming about what could be. We learn later, in various letters from Paul, how great those dreams are: that our limited understanding can't capture the peace created by God as we pray; that God is able to do immeasurably more than we could ask or imagine, and that God's paths are beyond anything we would be able to draft (Ephesians 3:20, Philippians 4:7, Romans 11:33). And yet, God's dreams did become tangible. In Ephesians we learn that we are God's dreams come true. We are tangible artifacts of the Creator, crafted in Christ Jesus for good works, which God planned in advance to be our way of life (Ephesians 2:10). Somehow God, before "the beginning," dreamt up this outlandish design for artwork that would, itself, do good work in and for the world. Then, in love, God decided to act on those dreams.

How might it have happened? We know from seventh grade physical science that work implies "a force overcoming resistance," so it involves the relatedness of more than one thing. From the start, God's dreams for a world must have included others. From the get-go, creation would necessarily be a place of community and relationship. And it would make sense that God would want for the "others"—the "good-workers" and all the other created things—to relate with that same love shared before time within the Trinity. Maybe this is what is meant in 1 John 4 when we read, "And so we know and rely on the love God has for us. God is love. Whoever lives in love lives in God, and God in them" (1 John 4:16 NIV).

Love's connectedness, then, seems to be the vision God has for creation. You can see this unfold later in our story as judges, prophets, and poets remind God's people of plans for them to seek the welfare of the city, to announce a year of jubilee in which debts are forgiven and property shared with families, to reconcile with violent enemies, and to give up empty religion in favor of caring for the poor. God seems to be creating, from the very beginning, with this in mind.

God was so enthralled with a life of loving connectedness that God loved into existence a world with the same potential. Like a painter setting out with an end in mind, God imagines and engineers a world continually unfolding as an expression of God's own original love. It's almost as if God were standing at the future, lovingly pulling creation forward.[17]

When I was in grade school we still watched films on reel-to-reel projectors. Whenever the film was over the teacher would have to put it in reverse to wrap the film back on the original reel in its correct order. Occasionally our teacher would rewind it through the projector, letting us watch the fast series of images as they flew by in reverse. Imagine seeing *God's Will, On Earth as It Is in Heaven*, the motion picture, on a film, but in reverse: First come the words "The End," followed by the camera focusing on a Tree called Life, whose leaves are for healing all nations and a voice saying, "Never again will anything be cursed." A love so powerfully magnetic that from the promised end of the long view "all things are new." Then this is the story as it unfolds: the Creator's loving dreams for the world residing in the future tumble backward through modern civilization as towers return to pastures and cathedral stones return to mountainsides. Then Jesus' commissioning breath to the apostles draws back into his mouth, the stone rolls back in place, and angels announce to sheep herders, "Peace on earth and goodwill on all with whom God's favor rests." Continuing in reverse through the destruction of Persian Empire, the great cedar beams come out of Solomon's temple and are rerooted along the shores of Lebanon; the Red Sea closes in front of the children of Israel; and the pyramids blow into mud and hay. That loving magnetic force, in reverse, looks like a flinging of life through history. The potential of all things traced back to their origins: cities into civilizations into small clans until there is less and less variety and everything is being drawn into the formless void and eventually into nothing, and into the beauty of love. And then the tape runs out, going flap, flap, flap, flap. . . .

The love at the end is the same love we find at the beginning, Alpha and Omega. The Great Imagineer begins by dreaming, by loving the future into an unfolding sustainable increasingly reconciled promised future destiny. Jesus preached of this destination as the kingdom of the heavens, or the kingdom of God, because it is home to that extended reach of God's loving intent.

Dream Journal exercise 2

Keep a notepad by your bedside this week. Set your alarm clock a bit earlier and leave a reminder to write whatever piece of your dreams fit on the page. Write what you can remember. You may need to get to bed earlier for a few nights to really get into deep dream sleep!

exercise 3 *Life's Dreams Journal*

Add thirty minutes before you go to bed a few times this week to journal on what you dreamed about during waking moments that day. Put the thirty minutes in your calendar right now so it is a priority. Write bits and pieces of what you dreamed about for your company, your family, your church, band, neighborhood association.

exercise 4 *Sketching God's Long View*

Clear a desk or table, grab some crayons or colored pencils and paper. Read the following three passages of Scripture and depict what is happening in them. Draw your own neighborhood or city or an international city you have visited as the modern context for these three Scriptures describing God's long view: Jeremiah 29:4–14; 1 John 4:7–18; Isaiah 43:16–21. Don't worry about being an artist, just mark stick figures and symbols on paper when it helps. Have fun with it.

(Wave 2 of 6)

God patiently *hovers*

And then the beginning happened: "God created the heavens and the earth. Now the earth was formless and empty, darkness was over the surface of the deep, and the Spirit of God was hovering over the waters" (Genesis 1:1–2 NIV). Sometimes the first step of creating is the most awkward one. It's an unfinished product, embarrassingly short of what we dreamed it would be, yet something more than we had before.

Imagine a baby being born to a man ready to pass along the family business. Imagine van Gogh's first strokes of paint. Imagine the homebuilder pouring a concrete foundation into those crudely dug holes. Imagine the high school band conductor meeting his freshman class on the first day: all the anticipation, all the realities of the risk and the yet-to-be-realized potential.

The earth was formless and void, and yet God didn't rush it. God, or more specifically, the Spirit of God, hovered.

Hovering is the creative posture of patience. No sooner had creation begun than the Spirit slowed the process down to what must have felt like a crawl. Watching like a hovering eagle. Nurturing like a nearby mother. This act of creative patience characteristic of artists repeats itself in God's story as it is told to us in Scripture. The Spirit that would hover over the chaotic void, would rest on Moses and the seventy elders, would fill the artisans of the tabernacle and the temple, would rest on the shepherd boy, singer-songwriter, David. This Spirit would hover over dozens of judges and prophets, and over Jesus as he went through his own rite of passage in the Jordan River with his cousin John.

The Spirit of God, also translated as "breath" in much of the Hebrew Old Testament, would course through shaped dirt until it became Adam. God's Spirit-breath would hover over the dead bones of Ezekiel's vision of Israel, and would come upon the Virgin Mary until she conceived Jesus. Jesus himself would have hovering patience. He would wait eighteen years between the boyhood dreams of his ministry as a teacher and healer at the temple and the day of his baptism, which signified his ministry's beginning at age thirty. Jesus would warn people not to rush things after some of his miracles, instructing them not to tell anyone what they saw. And, as we'll discover in later chapters, Jesus would "breathe" this Spirit on his followers, that they too would experience the peace and self-giving other-relatedness of God. This Spirit outfits Jesus' followers to do even greater things than he, to the point of even uttering words on their behalf when they don't know how or what to pray.

But each time the Spirit shows up, God's Spirit is hovering over the unexplored potential. God does not rush the process. From the very beginning of time as Scripture depicts it, we see the Spirit of God, as a patient artist, okay with the "unfinished" potential in the story. God is at home with things as they unfold.

Collage of Your Unfinished Context

exercise 5

What projects in your city, your house, your workplace, and your neighborhood are in unfinished states of progress? Take a camera with you today, drive around and take pictures of the unfinished projects. Send them to be developed or print them out on your computer. Next, do a Google-image search for images of doves, halos, and raindrops. Cut them out. Then, like the dove that hovered over Jesus, the halos that mark saints in icons and medieval paintings, and the rain that God sends to restore and renew the earth, glue or paste these images of the Spirit, still hovering today, over the unfinished things in your life.

(Wave 3 of 6)

God takes *risks*

Then God "moved out" of interrelatedness into other-relatedness. God moved out by taking action to make. Creation teaches us that (to use the words of my friend Todd Fadel) *love is concrete*.[18] The reverse of that is also true, as Cornel West emphasizes when he says that "justice is what love looks like in public." Loving moves into the physical realm, and when God's love goes public it is necessarily a design decision.

(Wave 3 of 6)

At this point God did something never done before. God spoke, "Let there be." Can you imagine the anticipation of the Triune God in that moment? As far as we know, never before had there been "something" besides God. What would happen? What would it look like? How soon would the experiment turn into the vision for "good-workers" to create alongside God?

The act of creativity requires a leap into the unknown, and God jumped out with enormous courage and imagination! We often domesticate the messiness of a creative God who entered into a space with no guarantees. We often suppose that creation for God was without risk because of theological commitments regarding God's knowledge of the future. But creativity necessarily requires the risk of mixing unknown conditions in order to see "newness" emerge. Can you just imagine that split fraction of time between the word *light* and the experience of light? What a huge leap into the unknown! What courage on God's part!

God's creation, as depicted across the narratives of Genesis, in the prayer dialogues with Job, and the new creation evoked by the resurrection of Jesus, are all acts of originality. They were unprecedented, and as such required a sort of risk. To rob these creative ventures of such risk is to flatten God's character, to dumb down the radical way in which God chose to make you and me and the world in which we move.

While in seminary I got the chance to become friends with Fred Wise, who describes himself as a painter of theological abstractions. After seminary Fred got a studio in Decatur and I'd drop in on him from time to time. One day I went to his little studio, a twelve-foot-square room in a warehouse he shared with sculptors, printers, and other painters. He had magazines everywhere, theology books and CDs and canvases in various stages of completion. I saw one that was filled with vermillion and ochre and other various browns and greens. It had both sharp edges and rounded edges. It looked like Hebrew letters were scribbled between the shapes. I could not figure out what this formless thing was, so I asked. He said casually, "I don't know yet."

Now, it never occurred to me that Fred's not knowing was due to some ignorance or finitude. He had a Masters in Fine Arts and a Masters in Divinity, had sold paintings for several thousands of dollars and had continued success for over twenty years. It never occurred to me that Fred didn't have a vision for why he had begun painting this one. In fact, when I asked further, he said he rarely knows what a painting "means" or "what it will look like" when he begins. And yet, he makes some of the most extraordinarily evocative paintings of landscapes and people, as well as beautiful abstract art. He makes these by just deciding to leap out on his hunches, and letting it play out from there.

I've found that most times when I'm asked to shorten the process of songwriting, being stingy with my time or resources, that the finished product feels forced or immature. Many a church leader, project designer, or group facilitator knows the struggle to work with groups who demand proof that a project is "probable" before beginning, lest we "waste" energy on something that might "fail." But according to the accounts in Genesis, God seemed comfortable taking unprecedented action. What incredible courage!

Prayers of Courage

exercise 6

Think of a friend or family member who has recently taken a huge risk, even if it didn't play out as they expected. On a blank sheet of paper write words that come to mind as you consider the courage they demonstrated. Repeat this by thinking of other personal examples of risk until you have generated a list of ten to twenty words. Don't try to organize the words, just write them randomly all over the page.

Now take those words and use them in a prayer to God. You may want to take a circle stencil and circle certain words and connect them like pictures of molecules connected to make various atoms.

Lastly, think of risks *you* have procrastinated on or have avoided. List these randomly across that same page and draw circles around them as well (you may want to use a different color here). Now, use lines to connect these possible risks with the risks that you have admired in others. Write along those lines words that represent whatever fears you have about taking these risks. *Perfect love casts out all fear.* Pray as you connect these, asking God to teach you how to connect the dots between loving dreams and concrete love, to risk reaching out, forgiving, and letting go your darlings or needs for external authority, prestige, wealth, or privilege.

(Wave 4 of 6)

God *listens* with us

It's amazing to picture the series of events following that initial risk when God spoke, "Let there be. . . . " One by one, day by day, session by session, life's unfolding continues in a way that foreshadows what is next. Maybe you've seen a potter do this. She grabs a lump of clay, throws it on the wheel, and begins to spin. After grabbing a little more slip, she presses her hands against the clay and watches it change. As she presses her thumb in, the clay stretches into a plate, or rises into a lip of a chalice, or broadens into the rim of a vessel. Only as it unfolds, each individual piece of clay, does the potter really know the shape, the characteristics it will take on, and what additional pieces it may require, be they arms, spouts, feet, stems, platters, what have you. I've heard potters describe this process as *listening to the material*. Songwriters and poets listen in similar ways; they sit with a subject as long as it takes, waiting for it to "speak to them."

As God's creative project unfolds, each session's work seems to speak to God as well about the next day's work. Waters beg for fish that would teem within them. Skies beg for fowl to stretch across them. And eventually the whole panoply cries out for creators, crafted with God's own characteristics, God's own image, capable of love, capable of being patient, able to dream, able to take risks and to listen.

Creation does speak. The hymns of Israel are filled with declarations attributed to everything from the mountains to the great sea monster to the cedars of Lebanon. Try reading the apostle Paul's take on the voice of creation from his letter to Jesus' followers in Rome. All creation, he writes, waits in eager expectation for the children of God (the good-workers) to come on the scene in their full, realized potential (Romans 8:19). And it would seem that God hears their longing just as much as Paul does.

It shouldn't be surprising that God would be listening to the creation being crafted. After all, God listens quite a bit in the stories we read elsewhere in Scripture. God listens to Abraham in negotiations over his nephew's corrupt town. God hears the praises of his people. In the great oppression under Egypt, God heard the cry of the Hebrew women, igniting the epic Exodus. We learn in the Gospels that Jesus himself heard a number of cries ranging from his mother at the wedding at Bethany, to the Roman centurion pleading for the health of his subordinate, to the gentile, Syrophoenician woman, to the thief next to him on the cross. Jesus would hear the cries of others. He would listen.

But the kind of listening we are talking about is not the same as acknowledging noise or words. It's what my friend, David McSween says is at the core of what it means to be an artist: perceiving. The potter, the poet, and the person who prays each have to read between such lines. They have to listen through to what is felt at the core. Jesus used a quote about this from Isaiah in defense of his use of parables. Some, he said "seeing they do not perceive, and hearing they do not listen, nor do they understand" (Matthew 13:13 NRSV). So what does it mean, then, that God listened?

My favorite story about listening comes from an interview by Dan Rather with Mother Teresa of Calcutta. Like most of us, amazed at her discipline and the results of her ministry, Rather wanted to know the secret of her prayer life. He asked, "When you pray, what do you say?" To this she responded, "I don't say anything, I just listen." So Rather, in his desire to find out the secret, continued and asked, "Well then, what does God say?" And Mother Teresa replied, "Oh, nothing, he just listens too." In Judeo-Christianity's earliest recorded acts of creation, we learn from God what mystics and artists have been teaching ever since: that making necessarily requires listening.

Listening Walk   exercise 7

Go to a nearby park or wildlife preserve with a camera, sketchpad, or journal. You are not going to write, sketch, or photograph much; this is more about prayer than representation. Pray for *eyes to see* and *ears to hear* God's good news today, before you take a walk. Then, don't rush things, just wait for something to catch your eye. Once you see it, walk around and look for the proper perspective. Sit or lean near that thing. Notice its shape, the color, the smell in the air, the textures, the lighting, even the sounds around you. Take three deep breaths and thank God for this beautiful part of creation unfolding in front of you. *This is the day that the Lord has made, so rejoice and be glad in it!* Look at the object with appreciation and gratitude, too. When you have settled in, let your pencil rest on the page or your eyes look through the lens of the camera, and consider what one thing this object of your attention has to say to you. Capture one sketch, short phrase, or photograph that says it best. Then breathe some more and pack up your stuff and enjoy the rest of your walk.

exercise 8   *Centering Prayer*

Find a place that is free from distraction and sit with God. You may want to begin by reading 1 Samuel 3:1–17 or 1 Kings 19:9–13. Then put your notes and books away. Start with a small amount of time—say fifteen minutes. Set a timer and then don't worry about the time. Sit in a chair with your feet flat on the floor and your hands on your legs, if you are able. Take several breaths. Listen. Don't fret if you don't hear anything. Listening and dismissing distractions helps sharpen your ears and eyes for God's abiding love that is near and drawing us into new creation.

(Wave 5 of 6)

God *reintegrates* each created thing with the rest of creation

This divine creative process from *dreaming* to *hovering* to *risking* to *listening* comes to a head when the new creation is introduced to the world. Newly created things are defined by their relationship to their environment. For example, a new vessel is placed on a counter with other vessels, or a plate is placed on a table with the rest of the setting. A song functions best as a piece of art when it is performed or recorded for others to hear it. Not because the song is a crude container of a core-message that must be received, but that music *becomes* once it vibrates the eardrum and soul of the listener.

In creative systems theory this stage of the process is often called *evaluation*. The flow of creativity unfolds when the creation emerges and is evaluated according to the internal set of rules set out by the creator. For example, a record producer is constantly making choices based on his perception of the intended audience, and yet the real test of the creative work is what happens when the song is actually released. Similarly, God's creative work is not complete until that goal of self-giving love is put to the test in community.

As the origins of heaven and earth are traced out in Genesis, we see that every new creation that emerges is defined by its relationship to the other creations. Since the moment that the heavens and earth were made, nothing existed in isolation. It is always the relationship of things that are being determined as they are created. God separated the light from the darkness, God separated the water under the expanse from the water above it, God called the waters to gather so that land could compliment them, God called the vegetation out of the land, God made celestial beings to separate day from night, God called teeming sea creatures out of the water, and living creatures out of the dry land to dwell in it, and God also created humanity to govern or steward over the other creatures. Each day of creation involved more nuanced relationships for those being created.

We learn in the second account of God's creative work (Genesis 2) that Adam is placed in the garden that God made, amid trees that were pleasing to Adam's eye and good for his nourishment. And we learn that woman is then invented by the Creator to introduce collaboration to the human condition. Not only that, but as the story unfolds, the voice of the creator would not come to Adam and Eve through a megaphone from some production trailer; God's "voice" would walk with them in the garden (Genesis 3:8 KJV).[19] Later, Noah, his family, and all of the young creation carried through the flood are joined together as beneficiaries of God's promise to put behind such violence by hanging up God's war bow in the sky. Abraham and Sarah, also, are called by God to connect with all the nations as blessings. Eventually Joseph would begin to realize this connection as he showed Egypt how to carry on a life of integration with the other nations, through saving and planning. And the Imagineer's long vision continues through the story of Scripture, as people are invited by the Creator into deeper relationship with the world around them. In spite of the sabotage that humanity exerts on God's interrelated world, the dreams of God prevail for a world that shares in that square dance of interconnectedness originating back to before time.

As the creation story and the book of Genesis trace the influx of more and more variety, like a cell splitting into two, differentiation is intended to bring more nuance and variety, not to create enmity between those parts. Even wolves and lambs are intended to lie down together, the poet Isaiah later teaches us. The infant is intended to play next to the asp's den. We learn in Ephesians that Jesus' life, death, and resurrection actually complete this vision, breaking down the walls of hostility, making the two one again. Every created thing is intended to be integrated with the other, as if the timeless square dance of God's Trinitarian love were the script for everything that God is making.

I know this part of the creative process may seem obvious—of course a created thing exists *next to* other created things—but it is easily overlooked. When God makes things, they have something to do with other things around them; they are never created simply for themselves. God's dream of birds has something to do with God's dreams for the air, and the God's dream of people has something to do with God's dreams for their good works amid the rest of creation. Similarly, the vision for good-workers would imply connection to others, and that connection would be similar to God's own loving connectedness. At this point in the creative process connection is put to the test. It's a simple lesson in sharing.

Now, fear can keep us from sharing what we've made. Fear, pride, and selfishness can disintegrate the intended harmony between what we make and the world for which we make it. Our own self-sabotaging fear blocks our visions for forgiveness and reconciliation. But God's perfect love casts out such fear. Perhaps this is why the early church would call the resurrection of Jesus on the Sunday following the Sabbath the Eighth day of creation. They would even build baptismal pools with eight sides to represent the new creation in Jesus, so that followers of Jesus would rise from waters of commitment into a new dawn of participatory life.

Countless epochs after the beginning, Jesus, Emmanuel, God-with-us, would serve as the curator, continuing God's creative intentions by reintroducing people to that intended world. Jesus would unpack from the texts of Isaiah, for example, the intentions for a humanity that would proclaim release to the captives, healing for the sick, and freedom for the enslaved. And he would breathe the Spirit on his followers, commissioning them to do even greater things than he. The relationships of creation would be reintegrated as Jesus would integrate law and prophets, demonstrate table practices with the outcast, love for one's enemies, and prayer for those who would harm him. In the first letter we have to the Corinthians, we learn that God will eventually place everything in harmony with Jesus' reign "so that God may ever be to them the All in All."[20]

Integration and Forgiveness   exercise 9

Take a piece of paper and fold it in half twice so that you have four quadrants. In the bottom right list your enemies: those who mean harm to you and your family; those who are politically opposed to what you are for; those who persecute you and others associated with your causes and passions. In the bottom left list your friends: advocates for those associated with your religious, political, or social causes. Write all of this so that both groups are at the bottom of the page, with only a crease separating them. Now draw a horizontal line to separate both groups from the empty top half of the page. Read Psalm 121, "I lift up my eyes to the hills—from where will my help come?"(NRSV) and imagine that the line you've drawn

' is a horizon line made by hills way off at a distance. Imagine your friends and your enemies looking into a future where Christ is reconciling all things to himself, where the separating walls between your two groups are healed and the grievances are forgiven through God's creative prowess. Pray for that magnetic field of God's promised reconciling future to pull both of you closer together as you approach those hills. Once you have completed this visual mapping prayer, read Ephesians 2:11–22 and consider the author's use of the words *near* and *far*.

(Wave 6 of 6)

God *rests*

God also rested!

Look out your window for a second. Drop your shoulders. Notice whatever tension you might be holding in your face and bring something to mind for which you are grateful or that could cause you to smile. Take a few deep breaths.

Something grossly overlooked in the creative process is the place of effortlessness, the place of play and imagination. It is not that God, after an eternity of unanxious Trinitarian fellowship, is exhausted by all the effort to create the earth and the galaxies and humanity in God's own image. Or is it? We don't know. What we do know is that God's lost art of creativity is a rhythm, and that this rhythm includes stopping, setting down the brush, the drumsticks, the pen, the shovel, closing the laptop, finishing the sermon, and turning off the iPhone. Dreams come during silence, play, and rest. But our projects, our toiling and laboring, and the work of making bricks for Pharaoh, or deadlines for the stockholders, or service orders for next week, or program reports for the heads of staff—all of this work can keep us from dreaming. And perhaps, God also wanted to get back to those dreams, so as not to lose a creative edge.

Today, church can keep us from dreaming. Church—when devoid of love, hovering, listening, risking, integration, or *rest*— can lose its creative edge as well. Jesus would recognize that his contemporaries were getting worn-out on the artificial rhythms of religion. He could see it in their eyes, and in the eyes of John's disciples, and the Pharisees. And in response he invited them into "the unforced rhythms of grace" (Matthew 11:29 MSG).

Grace is an interesting word for Sabbath rest. Grace frees us for all of these lost arts. Grace is the matrix, the canvas of creativity from Creation forward. Sabbath is the space where you open yourself to the pull of grace, the magnetic pull forward into the Imagineer's promised future. Like an artist designing her studio to accentuate deeper creative engagement, God quarters off a temporal place for creation to lean into grace. Grace and Sabbath are not places to brainstorm and plan for the next day, they are the opportunity to be here now, to taste and see that the Lord is good in this moment. Grace is that space where we look at one another and rediscover the words of Jesus, "The kingdom of God is in your midst" (Luke 17:21 NIV). Or as one scholar translates Jesus' words, "Unless a person submits to this original creation—the 'wind-hovering-over-the-water' creation, the invisible moving the visible, a baptism into a new life—it's not possible to enter God's kingdom" (John 3:5 MSG).

It is implicit from the remainder of the book of Genesis, the books to follow in the Hebrew and Christian scriptures, and the centuries of civilization since, that this first Sabbath was not God's retirement. God only ceased from work for that part of the creative process, and would then reenter the grand creative project. For storytelling purposes, the epoch of beginning may have come to a narrative peak, but many more beginnings would follow. The creative work of God would continue, and still continues. And so the creation of rest is a key component of the process.

As my friend Wayne Muller has written, "If we only stop when we are finished with all our work, we will never stop—because our work is never completely done. With every accomplishment there arises a new responsibility. . . . Sabbath dissolves the artificial urgency of our days, because it liberates us from the need to be finished."[21] In the instituting of Sabbath, God ordains the unfinishedness of the creature-creator relationship. God's patience, that unanxious loving presence, is a grace that resonates to this day. It is this unfathomable depth of peace, a "sense of God's wholeness" that stills all anxieties exhaled through "prayer and supplication with thanksgiving," to quote the apostle Paul's encouragement to the followers in the Way of Jesus in Philippi.[22] God's own competence regarding unfinishedness becomes the very vehicle for our own capacity to remain in the creature-creation relationship, whether that be me and God, or me and my creative projects.

What God makes on the seventh day is a place of promise, an environment free from anxiety, and a space to dream again. In practicing Sabbath, God made space for recreation.

Curating Unoccupied Spaces in Our Lives

exercise 10

Henri Nouwen has written that spiritual discipline requires preventing "everything in your life from being filled up. Discipline means that somewhere you're not occupied, and certainly not preoccupied." We have to "create that space in which something can happen that you hadn't planned or counted on."[23] This week, set aside a twenty-four-hour period for *play*. Plan time with family or friends. Plan ahead to have games on hand, musical instruments, drinks, or ingredients to cook a favorite or interesting recipe from scratch. Get your heart rate moving, get out of your planning mind, and be sure to laugh hard.

chapter 2

The Mediums of God's Artwork

Ten hours into the fifteen-hour trip from Charlotte to Boston in a cargo van covered in marathon and foot racing logos, surrounded by boxes of running shoes and T-shirts, I was long past any interest in the two cassette tapes we had or the 1 AM radio standards.

We pulled off on an exit north of Washington, DC, onto the Baltimore-Washington Turnpike. The exit was concrete grey, and had only two generic signs reading FUEL and RESTAURANT in late-sixties Federal Highway Administration font. We stopped the van to get gas, and the "pay here" gray room had no candies, no drinks, and no music playing. It felt like a scene out of *A Wrinkle in Time*—no color, no sound, no sense of place. I've since come to call this the Baltimore Feeling, that time at the end of vacation, an embarrassing lull in the conversation, a moment when I'm "on tilt" or "out of the flow." It is that surreal moment or environment when you feel cloudy, anything but surefooted, and uninspired.

Flash-forward fifteen years later to another encounter with feeling out of place. I was a new seminary graduate, in my first consulting experience. I was typing away feverishly in a coffee shop in Wilmington, Delaware, into my fifth trip north working with a large mainline congregation there. On this occasion, I skipped the morning worship gathering to prepare for a presentation to their staff and lay leadership. I had taught them most everything I could and had gotten in over my head trying to address systems issues.

I had plenty of caffeine in me, and had stayed up most of the night before, trying to get my ideas into manageable presentation slides. The week before I attended a three-day seminar on public presenting, so I was thinking hard—overthinking—about each step I needed to take to capture the attention of my audience.

Having pushed my preparation time to the very last moment, I closed my laptop and rushed to the church. I had cut it all too close, arriving less than ten minutes before the meeting was to start, still unsure of what I wanted to say, chest aching, head aching, short of breath, totally paralyzed by my fear of failure. Aware that I had jumped too far out of my league, I started into a rambling unrelated story about my two-year-old daughter wanting to fly like geese. I fumbled through the presentation, embarrassed, with little to offer them.

This second case was not one of understimulation, but one of overstimulation. Everything was amped up, the stakes felt too high, the tension between what I hoped for and what was possible was too great, and as a result nothing felt right. There was no space, no listening, seeing, or hearing.

When I first experienced that Baltimore Feeling all my senses were worn-out, nothing sounded good and nothing more could stimulate me. In the Wilmington Experience I had exhausted all my senses trying to prove myself and be someone I was not. Time and space had both become distorted in these cases.

But time and space are not always a source of resistance. How different it is when time is on your side, when the elements cooperate with you, when you're in the creative flow. To talk about God's creative process without examining how time, space, and matter conspire with God's artistic prowess would be to strip creation of its integrity, to overlook the contents that make any particular work of art shimmer. In this chapter we will look at the substance of art, the simple elements of time, space, and matter. These operate in the subtext of all art, as well as in the subtext of Hebrew and Christian Scripture, and they inform our views of God and God's realm.

Noticing
Your Context
exercise 11

Set aside twenty minutes to notice the time, space, and matter around you. Start by paying attention to your breath. Don't change your breathing, just notice the ins and outs. Next, begin to think through your five senses: First, notice the colors around you, the lighting, the reflections and shadows. Second, notice the sounds, including the hums of generators, the chatter of children, or background music. Can you hear your breath or your pulse? Third, notice the feelings of your body against the chair or stool you're sitting on, the feel of this book in your hands and each foot's contact with your sock and shoe and the surface of the floor and earth. Fourth, notice the smells. Are they bright, sour, stale? Last, notice the tastes in your mouth, at the tip of your tongue where sweetness is experienced, at the edges of your tongue where you taste sourness, at the back where saltiness and bitterness are experienced.

Artists Pay Attention to the Ingredients on the Box

Eddie's Attic has a flight of stairs you walk up, passing layers of vintage posters from Americana bands to handmade promotions for new indie songwriters. When you get to the top of the stairs and pay your cover, you head into the Listening Room, complete with a bar, about thirty various chairs and tables, and space for another forty people to stand.

This legendary Atlanta venue is the type of rare place where singer-songwriters love to play because the audience comes purposefully to listen, to get drawn in. In graduate school I would often play Eddie's with my cellist friend, Bill Davis. We played open mic songwriter contests and occasional hour-long shows. Half of the fun was getting to know other songwriters and learning about the craft of writing. One man in particular, in his fifties, would listen closely to my set and then pull up a stool next to me at the bar and mention other artists I should listen to from week to week. He turned me on to Townes Van Zandt, and Leonard Cohen, and reintroduced me to Roy Orbison and the Beatles. He said that every song has some basic ingredients, and that listening to what I played he could tell what I had been listening to while writing. He said it was like looking on the side of the cereal box for the ingredients. Knowing what is inside your food changes the way you eat.

What popular movements like whole food, slow food, locavores, and garden-to-table foodies are reclaiming is this same sort of awareness—of a meal's ingredients—and how your food's origin affects your whole life. When you start paying attention to what's in your food, you'll find your diet, your cravings, your cooking, even your attention to waste and land use changing. What and how you eat affects what you make, and the life you make as well. Art is like life in this way: the raw ingredients, the various materials and mediums that you intentionally engage with, affect the art you make. This kind of attention is a key element of all kinds of art.

What my friend at Eddie's Attic realized is that the ingredients have a necessary influence on the art. The choice of materials, and the fashioning of them, matters almost as much as the artist's eye or creative process.

In the last chapter we explored how God's artistry unfolds in six wave cycles, from the beginning and in time ever since: *dreaming > hovering > risking > listening > reintegrating > resting*. I've proposed this way of seeing God's work so that we, who have been made in God's image, can better acquaint ourselves with some of these lost arts. Dreams, when articulated, reward the one who hovers over them, lending courage to risk, which begs even deeper attentiveness. When this is done well, creativity expresses itself as harmony between the newly formed objects, eventually freeing up the imagineer to rest and dream again. Dreaming, hovering, risking, listening, reintegrating, and resting all describe a creation process, but this description leaves out the raw materials, the ingredients to God's creative project.

Focusing on process alone would be like describing a painter without talking about choices in pigments and canvas, without asking about the use of perspective, color, or tone, and with no attention to the place or day and age in which he painted. It's like an actor reading a script cold, no background story, no research, no setting, posture, accent, or pathos. Attention to process is enriched when we pay as much attention to the ingredients. It's the difference between knifing out the square mold of fast-food jelly from a plastic container to drag over buttered white toast, and spreading my mother's homemade strawberry-rhubarb jam across the toasted edges of her oven-warm homemade sourdough bread. In art, as in life, the stuff we use to make our creations matters.

Life Is Made of Stuff, Footprints, and Moments

When we consider what artists make we usually describe material stuff like a painting, a building, a dress, a sculpture, or a book. And this stuff is made of other stuff: dresses from fabric, buildings from bricks and mortar, paintings from paint and canvas, books from ink and paper. But artists fashion more than stuff; they must also make intentional decisions about their footprint, the impact of their stuff in any given environment. A dancer carefully graphs out the where and how of her body in coordination with other bodies and other stuff. Then, stuff and the associated footprints must be coordinated into moments of time.

A composer and conductor bring musicians into time with each other. Their raw materials (horn, wind, even various notes or pitches) do not mean that the art is necessarily experienced until placed into measured moments of time. And so it is that in creating heaven, earth, and the rest of the cosmos, God also makes their raw materials: moments, stuff, and footprints.

Somehow, God, the Imagineer who "was and is and is to come," transcends time, space, and matter, existing as communion of love since before the beginning. And granted, who-knows-how-many years later the church would argue that God's unique creative genius includes the capacity to make all out of nothing. But only seconds after something came out of nothing, love would become more and more concrete as God continued crafting something out of something.

Love was made manifest by adjoining itself to the here-and-now as the stuff, footprint, and actual moments of creation were put into play in the hands of God's crafting. I'm not splitting hairs; the nuance that I'm getting after is that God's creating project has always been about God-with-us (Emmanuel) as opposed to some bubble-boy version of God where nothing crafted could actually come into contact with God's loving self. Eugene Peterson paraphrases the familiar John 1:14 by saying, "The Word became flesh and blood and moved into the neighborhood" (MSG). This is the magic of the Son of God inside the dynamic created world, claiming that the dreams of God fit here and now. And all the way back to creation we see God all up in the here and now of the neighborhood's business.

God was not content to compose a symphony to be played on a synthesizer. God went farther than a make-believe universe that only "appears" free but is really a puppet, an emanation of God's dreams. God's creative work moved toward deeper characteristics of embodied, genuine, and organic by handing the score over to material beings, making creation's symphony a living and breathing thing. And so light, dark, animals, mushrooms, tidal pools, and humans would all come into existence, endowed by their creator with their necessary roles within God's song. Like a bell or a piano string, it's their physical vibrations that make their tone audible.

Ignatian Prayer
with Creation   exercise 12

St. Ignatius of Loyola, who lived in the sixteenth century, taught people to read Scripture while imagining themselves inside the story. Grab a Bible and read Genesis 2:4–25 while reflecting on the role of time, space, and matter in the creative life. Imagine yourself inside that story, working through each of your five senses of touch, smell, sight, hearing, and taste. You don't necessarily need to be a character in the story, though you can be. Journal or sketch what you notice.

chapter 3

Stuff: Material Reality

We can be amazed at the feat of coordination that God underwent bringing matter, space, and time into harmony. But perhaps we can more deeply understand these separate elements animated by God's creative venture if we examine them one by one. Let's begin with matter, the stuff of which everything is made.

Craft making has become increasingly popular with the Do-It-Yourself generation. We realize that with the right materials and right training, amateurs can build things that are useful and have a sense of homespun, indigenous originality. YouTube channels are devoted to passing craft know-how to the curious novice.

My wife is a scrapbooker, and for a while we owned a scrapbooking store with a few other friends. The key to scrapping, as with most crafts, is to think of the story you want to tell and to allow that story to inform your choice in materials. Materials such as paper, stamps, inks, and photos all say something. Choosing what you use is as essential to the artistic process as the skills of cutting and layout. So what materials did our Creator pull together when it came time to bring the dream into reality?

In Genesis 2, like a second camera angle, or a behind-the-scenes documentary, we get an intriguing glimpse into another perspective on Creation. While in the more popular first chapter of Genesis we are given a description of the process God undertook, in chapter 2 the text emphasizes the recipe for creation—the ingredients of God's project:

> These are the generations of the heaven and of the
> earth when they were created, in the day that the Lord
> God made earth and heaven.
>
> No shrub of the field was yet in the earth, and no herb
> of the field had yet sprung up; for the Lord God had not
> caused it to rain upon the earth, and there was not a
> man to till the ground; but there went up a mist from the
> earth, and watered the whole face of the ground. Then
> the Lord God formed man of the dust of the ground,
> and breathed into his nostrils the breath of life; and man
> became a living soul. And the Lord God planted a garden
> eastward, in Eden; and there He put the man whom He
> had formed. And out of the ground made the Lord God
> to grow every tree that is pleasant to the sight, and good
> for food; the tree of life also in the midst of the garden,
> and the tree of the knowledge of good and evil. (Genesis
> 2:4–9 JPS)

This version of the creative story emphasizes the stuff God used
to make us and the world within which God placed the earliest
humans.

When Jesus walked among us he would teach about God's
purposes existing in the world like yeast exists in bread. Jesus
rejected the idea that God's will exists simply as an idea or
strategic plan that looks great on paper. God's will, like art,
exists in its accomplishment. He taught his disciples to pray
that God's will would be accomplished in the created realm
of earth as it is accomplished in God's realm of heaven. God's
will is his identity, his intention, and as such, God's character is
based in this intention being manifest. Jesus loved to get nitty-
gritty about the completed stuff of life that God intended.

As in the Genesis 1 account, God is the only character
introduced in the beginning of the Genesis 2 creation story.
Then God molds dirt into a human shape and breathes life into
us. It's clear here that the creative process begins before breath

was added, but that living stuff has an intimate relationship with God's breath. The breath of God (*ruach* in the original Hebrew) shows up throughout Scripture. Its moisture spreads the traces of God's DNA all around creation. In the case of this story, God-breath transforms dirt into a living human:

> Then the LORD God formed man of the dust of the ground, and breathed into his nostrils the breath of life; and man became a living soul. (Genesis 2:7 JPS)

The poetry of the Hebrew is playful. Only the slightest gesture changes *dust* to *man*. The Hebrew word for "dirt," *ha-adam*, gets introduced by the definite article *the* and suddenly changes into the proper noun *adam,* or "man." And so you basically have the entrance of our second character, Mr. Dirt-n-Breath, or human.

From that point forward God's breath will continue to show up as a life-giving miracle. In Ezekiel the dried bones of deceased Israel are breathed into life again by God. In the upper room after his resurrection, Jesus appears in the midst of the women and men saying, "peace be with you" and then breathes the Spirit on them. In John's revelation the dead and decaying prophets are breathed with new life. The material world, the stuff of which you and I are made, is designed to hold God's DNA; it is the created home for Spirit breath.

Various other faith systems and certain forms of Christianity have tried throughout history to say that the material universe is an unspirited place. And yet God, "in whom and through him we all have our being," is animating everything—all stuff—into what it is. Matter matters to God!

Noticing the Stuff within God's Art

exercise 13

Before we go on, look at the stuff around you. What is it made of? Is the counter or sofa near you made of wood? If so, do you know what kind of wood? Ash, oak, mahogany? Can you imagine the mountain that held the granite under your feet, or the great tree from which the beams and rafters around you were hewn? What colors are used on the walls around you? How many different textures can you identify around you? Are there coarse as well as supple things nearby? Look around you for something that you regard as holy. Why is it holy? What marks something as holy to you?

Footprints: The Land, Space, and Our Reach

> *Love all God's creation, the whole and every grain*
> *of sand in it. Love every leaf, every ray of God's light.*
> *Love the animals, love the plants, love everything. If you*
> *love everything, you will perceive the divine mystery in*
> *things. Once you perceive it, you will begin to understand*
> *it better every day. And you will come at last to love the*
> *whole world with an all-embracing love. . . . All is like an*
> *ocean, all is flowing and blending: a touch in one place*
> *sets up movements at the other ends of the earth ... If*
> *you strike here, something somewhere will wince.*
>
> —Father Zossima in Dostoevsky's *The Brothers*
> *Karamazov* [24]

God, who has committed as a craftsman to the medium of this world, then constructs that material into an environment for the human. We were given a hint that context was important when the narrator began Genesis 2 describing the world as it was before there was "man to till the ground." Before God's created image-bearer was tending after matter, the matter existed. The text reads like the setting notes in a play script: "No plant or animal life, just a mist watering the face of the ground."

This biblical description of space in the beginning is detailed and rooted in physical reality. Often when we talk about space, our minds move into more ethereal and nebulous places. For our artistic purposes, however, I want us to think of space as our reach, as the area we walk around in, and the footprint of our work. Much talk lately around being "green" emphasizes the benefits of having a light or small footprint, implying the negative impact of our actions on the environment. But our feet leave prints on any and every path we take. And influence does not always corrupt, it can also nurture, heal, and bless. Just think of the footprints of Thomas Edison and Frank Lloyd Wright on Chicago, of Martin Luther King Jr. on Atlanta, or a resident's influence on his neighborhood and a mother's influence on her children. A dancer or gymnast is intentional about her footprints. And so the artist takes responsibility for a certain space, and influences that space by thinking intentionally about how to use it.

After making Mr. Dirt-n-Breath, God plants a garden in a particular space, in the east between four mighty rivers. And God places our protagonist within it to live.

Settings are significant intentional choices to artists. Take, for example, the setting of the movie classic *Casablanca*. Rick Blaine and Ilsa Lund meet up in Morocco, a war escapist's fantasy getaway that is coming under military occupation. Had the writers picked another more horrific war-torn location or more secure luxurious place, the story would not have carried the memorable drama of those two lovers and probably would not have won the Epstein brothers and Howard Koch their Academy Awards for best writers. Another example is the Beatles' breakthrough song, "Eleanor Rigby." Her picking up the rice "in the church" tells a story of loneliness in and of itself, the way picking up paper in front of a museum would never do.

And so *ha-adam* is flanked by orchards at the head of four mighty rivers, near a source of precious metals and the great rivers of Egypt, in an untouched young verdant garden:

> And the LORD God planted a garden eastward, in Eden; and there He put the man whom He had formed. And out of the ground made the LORD God to grow every tree that is pleasant to the sight, and good for food; the tree of life also in the midst of the garden, and the tree of the knowledge of good and evil. And a river went out of Eden to water the garden; and from thence it was parted,

and became four heads. The name of the first is Pishon; that is it which compasseth the whole land of Havilah, where there is gold; and the gold of that land is good; there is bdellium and the onyx stone. And the name of the second river is Gihon; the same is it that compasseth the whole land of Cush. And the name of the third river is Tigris; that is it which goeth toward the east of Asshur. And the fourth river is the Euphrates. And the LORD God took the man, and put him into the garden of Eden to dress it and to keep it. (Genesis 2:8–15 JPS)

Environments matter deeply to the Creator because they evoke a tone; environments can serve to limit or expand possibility.

Consider, also, how environments affect everyday life. Have you ever walked into the middle of a hard conversation between friends and felt the tension in the room? Or have you ever noticed how different spaces are better suited for different conversations? It is awkward to talk about the mountains or fishing or gardening in the middle of the mall. Likewise, it is easier to lose yourself in music or sports in a large arena or crowded bar as opposed to a small group meeting in a living room. Or maybe you've noticed the benefits of studying in a room with a window or with some green in it, versus in an enclosed gray room with florescent lights.

Engineers, architects, and designers are bringing into modern popular conversation the discipline of "built environments." Like the Eastern students of feng shui, Western environmental engineers understand that certain heights, proportions, colors, and textures affect those within the room. And design sciences around built environs has influenced everything from the ways that paint swatches are sold at Lowes to the way chairs are set up in community organizing events.

It shouldn't come as a surprise, then, that God has an interest in built environments. Scripture gives us a look into the detailed architectural elegance of Noah's ark, the Tabernacle,

Solomon's Temple, and even the New Jerusalem depicted in John's Revelation. Take, for example, the book of Ezekiel. In it we learn that this priest was given elegant, grandiose dimensions and precious materials precisely to awaken in the reader dimensions and scales evocative of glory. In a vision, God transported Ezekiel from captivity to a high mountain back home in the land of Israel:

> To the south there were buildings that looked like a city. [God] took me there and I met a man deeply tanned, like bronze. He stood at the entrance holding a linen cord and a measuring stick.
>
> The man said to me, "Son of man, look and listen carefully. Pay close attention to everything I'm going to show you. That's why you've been brought here. And then tell Israel everything you see."
>
> First I saw a wall around the outside of the Temple complex. The measuring stick in the man's hand was about ten feet long. He measured the thickness of the wall: about ten feet. The height was also about ten feet.
>
> He went into the gate complex that faced the east and went up the seven steps. He measured the depth of the outside threshold of the gate complex: ten feet. There were alcoves flanking the gate corridor, each ten feet square, each separated by a wall seven and a half feet thick. The inside threshold of the gate complex that led to the porch facing into the Temple courtyard was ten feet deep.
>
> He measured the inside porch of the gate complex: twelve feet deep, flanked by pillars three feet thick. The porch opened onto the Temple courtyard.
>
> Inside this east gate complex were three alcoves on each side. Each room was the same size and the separating walls were identical.

He measured the outside entrance to the gate complex: fifteen feet wide and nineteen and a half feet deep.

In front of each alcove was a low wall eighteen inches high. The alcoves were ten feet square.

He measured the width of the gate complex from the outside edge of the alcove roof on one side to the outside edge of the alcove roof on the other: thirty-seven and a half feet from one top edge to the other.

He measured the inside walls of the gate complex: ninety feet to the porch leading into the courtyard.

The distance from the entrance of the gate complex to the far end of the porch was seventy-five feet.

The alcoves and their connecting walls inside the gate complex were topped by narrow windows all the way around. The porch also. All the windows faced inward. The doorjambs between the alcoves were decorated with palm trees. (Ezekiel 40:2–16 MSG)

Like a software programmer reading code and commenting, "How elegant," so the educated priestly class, Ezekiel's earliest audience, would be swept away by the symmetry, scale, and detail of the "shaped environment" laid out for God's glory.

One of the most profound examples of God's intention with the footprint or spatial impact of creation came when a refugee rancher was watching his father-in-law's goats. This political refugee (someone with no space) had run away after killing a national in a totalitarian government where he had been adopted and naturalized as a citizen. Four decades had passed since then, and now, as a middle-aged man, while performing his routine goat-herding work, something caught his eye. The Scriptures tell us he "turned aside," and when he did, he saw something unusual: a shrub or small desert tree was roaring with flames, without burning up. When he approached the burning bush, a voice called him out by name, "Moses, Moses."

What followed were careful instructions to step out of his sandals, because the very ground beneath his feet had been declared holy.

This God would reveal himself to Moses as "I Am," or "YHWH," the God of his foreparents; the God who centuries earlier had told Abram and Sari how God would make them into a blessing-shaped nation by preparing a land, a place, for that nation. God continued, instructing Moses that God's mission was to transplant the Israelites into a better space, a better environment.

> "I have come down
> to rescue [the Israelites] from the hand of Egypt,
> to bring it up from that land
> to a land, goodly and spacious,
> to a land flowing with milk and honey,
> to the place of the Canaanite and Hittite."
> (Exodus 3:8 FBM)[25]

So God sends Moses from one place to another place, where Egypt's oppressive hand cannot reach, plentiful with space, where nurture and sweetness flow like river water. After this commission Moses interrupts God, voicing his insecurities about confronting Pharaoh, to which YHWH responds:

> "Indeed, I will be-there with you,
> and this is a sign for you that I myself have sent you:
> when you have brought the people out of Egypt,
> you will (all) serve God by this mountain.
> (Exodus 3:12 FBM)

God took a displaced refugee, woke him up to God's present reality in an unknown place, and then tied Moses' mission to transplanting the people of Israel from one unhealthy place to another more nurturing place. And the very proof to people that Moses was sent by God would be the right use of that place in the foreseeable future, worshipping as a community on the holy-space where Moses had first removed his sandals. God chose the ground that would be hallowed in God's encounter with Moses and God set apart a spacious land for a life of worship.

The Psalms, the Hebrew songbook, returns to this vision of land over and over, as a built environment, designed to hold God's glory:

> His abode has been established in Salem,
>> his dwelling place in Zion. (Psalm 76:2 NRSV)

> Surely his salvation is at hand for those who fear him,
>> that his glory may dwell in our land.
>> (Psalm 85:9 NRSV)

> For the LORD hath chosen Zion;
>> He hath desired it for His habitation:
> "This is My resting-place for ever;
>> here will I dwell; for I have desired it.
> I will abundantly bless her provision;
>> I will give her needy bread in plenty.
> Her priests also will I clothe with salvation;
>> and her saints shall shout aloud for joy."
>> (Psalm 132:13–16 JPS)

Today we hear countless reports about wars over holy land, fought to protect or defend a certain place. But God didn't haphazardly declare a small percentage of land holy as a scarce exception to the rest of a profane creation. Rather, like a painter shading the background of a landscape, God set apart a place where Israel's art of life was to play out. God picked the holy way in which the holy land would be used or cultivated. God showed Moses how to honor that place of meeting, by turning aside and by removing his sandals.

Psalm 132 shows us God as an environmental engineer, choosing the space that would cradle Israel's footprint. God sets apart that place for nourishment to the poor and for faith practices. God declares a place that would ring God's song, with literal "shouts of joy." Cultivating an environment, honoring a certain place by taking off our sandals, calling a land home, nourishing the poor, and honoring the blessed fruitfulness of all that was created before us, these are all acts of faith rooted to space.

Centuries after God's promises of land to Abram and Moses, Jesus would teach that the "disinherited in spirit" inherit God's realm, and that the meek inherit the land:

> "Blessed are the poor in spirit, for theirs is the kingdom of heaven." (Matthew 5:3 NRSV)

> "You're blessed when you're content with just who you are—no more, no less. That's the moment you find yourselves proud owners of everything that can't be bought." (Matthew 5:5 MSG)

Our art-of-life awakens us, like the refugee-rancher Moses, to the hallowed space that our footprints make; awakening us in ways that others may never be able to learn, so long as we remain "copious in spirit." The meek and the poor in spirit are able to understand the place of God in *this* world.

Wendell Berry is a farmer, poet, and essayist who has committed to the agrarian life of his family farm in Kentucky. He writes in his poem "History" that he began his farm life as an intentional choice, as his "art of being here."[26] Berry wanted that place to "instruct his wants" in such a way that they would "belong together" and be inextricably tied to that very "place." Almost like the children of Israel on their reorienting journey out of oppression into a life of freedom, Berry writes, "Until my song comes here / to learn its words, my art / is but the hope of song."[27]

In chapter 1, we discussed the rare interrelatedness between the potter and her clay as characteristic of the listening part of the creative process. Berry is describing a similar, intimate relationship—but to land. And this interrelatedness is echoed in the texts we've read from Genesis and the Psalms where the very land that God fashions, the space under God's influencing footprint, instructs God's own "art of being here."

Jesus, in fact, taught a lot about space. In his dialogue with Philip and Thomas at their last shared Passover supper, before he famously said, "I am the Way," Jesus described that he was going ahead of his disciples to "prepare a place" (John 14). When the disciples were anxious about getting to that place without Jesus as their trailblazer, Jesus comforts them with the words that he is the trail. What if that trail did, in fact, lead to a prepared setting? What if Jesus wanted the disciples to know through creative intentionality, just as he had, a spacious world of burning bushes? A place where God "dwells" the way Psalms 76, 85, and 132 describe God dwelling in the land. A place where we would "do even greater things" than Jesus (John 14:12). A place that would inform our "art of being here." Jesus expounded on this with the disciples by explaining that he "must leave" in order for his followers to most deeply inhale the Spirit's reliable breath and "realize" that Jesus dwells in his Father, and we in Jesus, and Jesus in us.

New Testament scholar Tom Wright describes this transformed space this way: "We could cope—the world could cope—with a Jesus who ultimately remains a wonderful idea inside his disciples' minds and hearts. The world cannot cope with a Jesus who comes out of the tomb, who inaugurates God's new creation right within the middle of the old one."[28] Jesus' death and resurrection were moments that refashioned time, space, and matter into deeper participation with God's dreams.

The physical land, the very ground on which we stand, was recreated in Christ's reversal of death and its power. The spatial demarcation between what Jews regarded as commonplace and the "holiest of holies" was removed when the temple curtain was torn. Matthew's telling of Jesus' resurrection even includes reports of the dead from underground walking again in the land of the living. And then, in the Acts of the Apostles, we encounter followers of Jesus refashioning space and matter in the same way as Jesus. This sect of Jews would share God's promises beyond the geographical bounds of the promised land, changing economic practices in Corinth, changing panhandling zones into centers for healing, and turning prisons into halls of sung worship in Philippi. In John's apocalyptic telling of the completion of God's grand work of art, he describes a New Jerusalem located in a newly fashioned heaven and earth. Reading those early reports, you can almost hear the echoes of Jesus' words, "even greater things than these," as the disciples take their footprints seriously, first in Jerusalem, and then on to the ends of the earth and the ends of time.

Noticing Your Reach within God's Artwork

exercise 14

Take another breath, slowly stretch out your arms, and see how far you can reach. Slowly and deliberately stretch one up and the other down. Bring them together around your head and back. What tools do you have around you that could extend your reach? How does a pencil, a computer, a smart phone, a car, or even a bank account extend your reach? Now, investigate the space around you and consider what spaces God might be able to reach. Notice the place under your feet and wiggle your toes. Perhaps even slip your shoes off for a moment and feel the floor. Imagine God's glory actively involved in the place where you are standing or sitting. Imagine God's glory manifest in the tools of your life the way that Moses' staff became a participant in the liberation story of Israel. Consider this place holy. Consider those extensions of your reach holy. Dedicate them to God's use.

Time: Being in the Moment

Calling, it waits for the hour when the soul shall open itself, having found its God and its home. When this is so, the soul will not keep its wealth to itself, but will let it flow out into the world. Wherever love proceeds from us and becomes truth, the time is fulfilled.
—Eberhard Arnold[29]

Any work of art employs matter, space, and *time*. Eberhard Arnold, founder of the Bruderhof ("place of brothers") Communities, an early-twentieth-century iteration of the modern intentional community movement, wrote that our calling is intricately connected to time. He wrote that the Creator's purpose for time is fulfilled the moment that "love proceeds from us" (similar to what we've already noted about the creating Trinity). Time is both destination (home/truth) and procession (sharing/flowing). It can be understood from many perspectives. We often confuse timing with linear sequence, but we'll see that in art—as in much of life—time has more to do with moments than with hands on the clock. Timing is everything, as comics and actors say.

My friend Sherra is part of an improv class that meets every Tuesday night. They talk about timing in interesting ways. She once explained how improv timing works, that the timing of a joke has to do with the comedian being "in the moment." Instead of worrying about what line is next, the actor plays each line like a tennis ball coming over the net, one at a time, waiting to see what happens. Comedic timing is less about "when" and more about awareness of "what's happening right now."

In my work with churches and in our inner-city neighborhood I've become a huge fan of community organizing tools that help groups focus on the moment. One in particular is called *Theory U*, developed by organizer Otto Scharmer.[30] Based on focus groups and interventions with groups ranging from South Africa's Truth and Reconciliation Commission to German healthcare professionals, Scharmer and others explain the importance of moving from point A to B, through a process called *presencing*, intentionally being present in a posture of trust. Imagine a rubber band stretched between two points, such as nails on a board. When left alone it makes ———————— a straight line. Remember that geometry adage "the shortest distance between two points is a straight line"? Well, the natural temptation in change management is to find a leader who can get the group there in the shortest time. *Theory U* suggests that the most effective, lasting change requires more time and attention than a straight line, so rather than a straight line, imagine you pulled the rubber band down from the two nails: it would form an upside down U. "Moving down the left side of the U is about opening up and dealing with the resistance of thought, emotion, and will; moving up the right side is about intentionally reintegrating the intelligence of the head, the heart, and the hand in the context of practical applications."[31]

Scharmer teaches that building a U: flowing downward together from A and then upward together to B, brings deeper, more effective change. Similar to the way a comedian needs to be aware of the moment, unencumbered by two or three moves ahead, a community change agent is most effective when aware of the moment, free from the anxiety of an outcome or solution.

According to *Theory U*, the way in which groups attend to situations determines the outcome. Community organizing is about building trust. Without establishing trust, people encounter each other based on their anxieties about an unknown future, or their prejudices from past experiences. Individuals or parties who meet without entrusting the present moment to one another are limited to what they already believe or want, making the interaction more like *combat* than *discovery*. It would be like band members with no score and no way to hear or see one another. You've got to get folks where they can hear or see each other, and establish a common page to work from. The facilitator's job in *Theory U* is to create a new, shared experience in real time that suspends individuals' past and future biases. They call this "building the container."

Think of team-building events you've participated in, such as rope courses or trust falls, where members of a group learn to trust one another. Now move beyond physical trust to include confession, curiosity, sharing emotional fears. Moving out of chronological time and into the moment is the time-space where playful brainstorming and the freedom to create as a community exists.

You can see this in Jesus' conversations with Peter at the shore after the resurrection. He asks Peter the same question over and over, "Do you love me?" And each time he is giving Peter the chance to go deeper and deeper with his response. Like the unanxious Sabbath presence of God amid an unfinished creation, Jesus is free to remain attentive to Peter, even when he knows he will shortly be leaving Peter and his other disciples. In community organizing, this process of revisiting our assumptions about each other, the process of seeing each other with more and more depth, leads to a place of safety.

The safety of love and trust is not always the result of the space (classrooms and coffee shops can work as well as a monastery or campground). The unique character of every "safe container" is the moment in time. It's like a great concert, a good conversation, a slow meal with old friends, or making love with your spouse when you step back and ask, "Where did the time go?" You were basically so present tense, so *in the moment* that time conspired with you.

Jesus' stories about watchfulness echo the idea of losing yourself in the moment. He would teach the importance of "knowing the times." Jesus would challenge his followers to "choose this day whom you will serve." Referencing the life of the sparrow, he would encourage us to not "fret about what tomorrow holds." He told stories about maidens with spare lantern oil on hand late at night and their wicks trimmed and ready. He would warn about people pulled, unaware, into God's dreams from their plows in the field. Even his prayer for the disciples at Gethsemane were that they would "watch and pray." Jesus knew that God was building a container—sanctifying space and time, for God's dreamed-for art project. And knowing that this is where the "action would be," so to speak, Jesus wanted to draw the disciples into such transformational moments when time would be on their side.

But time does not always seem to conspire with us. As in both my Baltimore Feeling and Wilmington Experience (look back to chapter 2), time can seem relentlessly long or ruthlessly scarce. Irish mystic John O'Donohue has said that "stress is a perverted relationship with time." Like the Salvador Dali painting *The Persistence of Memory*, we see time melting away as we work harder and harder to control or own it. And so our lives, like bad sitcoms or flat script readings, become less improvisational, and more predictably about getting from one punch line to the next.

The difference that creatives feel between a sense of timelessness and a sense that time slipping away has been a topic of inquiry for ages. After three decades of research studying how artists and other innovative, creative people reach "optimal experience," psychologist Mihaly Csikszentmihalyi distilled his findings into a theory he calls "Flow." He describes it as "being completely involved in an activity for its own sake. The ego falls away. Time flies. Every action, movement, and thought follows inevitably from the previous one, like playing jazz. Your whole being is involved, and you're using your skills to the utmost."[32] This is that unforced moment where time meets calling, and it is where the stressful relationships with time are stripped away.

Time in a Bottle

> *Our problem today [is that] the space for imagination to expand and take shape is inversely proportional to the speed at which we live. Driven hard and fast, we lack the time to allow alternate worlds and possibilities to form, careening past small turnings and exits, bound to follow the obvious straight paths of the present arrangement. Yet if we stop and wait, and close our eyes to the buy now, take me now images, we will begin to remember, new worlds will form and new exits will become apparent. Before change . . . comes waiting.*
> —Walter Brueggemann [33]

In computer programming, self-employed folks who work from home use all sorts of ways to trick themselves into getting things done on time. They recognize that unstructured time does not always equal freedom to create. One trick they use is called time boxing. Like a lawyer or therapist who bills by the hour, they restrict their work into limited sessions. Have you ever been in meetings that never seem to end, that get hijacked by chatty colleagues, or never seem to reach actionable next steps within the specified time? Instead of avoiding unproductive planning meetings, time boxing constrains the time, and participants learn to budget accordingly. For example, you might begin a meeting with a commitment to leave the table no more than twenty minutes later. After a few meetings, participants learn to surface issues more quickly and to work toward measurable actions within a designated time.

One evolution of time boxing was invented by Italian programmer Francesco Cirillo.[34] While in college, he noticed how much his concentration and passion for work ebbed and flowed between the adrenaline-driven final papers and all-nighters to the doldrums of early-semester drudgery. Cirillo wondered if he could stay in the flow because those moments were apportioned into small, simple time frames. So he grabbed an old tomato-shaped kitchen timer and dared himself to focus only on the work for ten minutes straight as if it were the only ten minutes he had to devote to the task. Gradually this practice grew into twenty-five-minute segments.

The simple Pomodoro (Italian for "tomato") Technique that Cirillo has taught since 1998 requires practitioners to guard complete twenty-five-minute indivisible "Pomodoros" of focus using a timer. If someone calls during a Pomodoro, you wait to call back until the five-minute break between Pomodoros. If you think of an urgent task, you write it down and continue until your Pomodoro is over. Say your mother keeps calling or your husband is heading home with a sick child and you absolutely have to stop. Fine! You consider that uncompleted Pomodoro as spoiled, and return to a fresh twenty-five-minute Pomodoro when the interruption is over. This sort of time boxing helps the person get better at estimating how long something will take, and to devote full attention when they need to be in the flow. Time becomes manageable and you can get realistic about your time commitments.

If you look at the use of time in Scripture, you can see how God's creative work is described in a way similar to time boxing. Many scholars see how the days of creation noted in the book of Genesis are poetry designed to evoke order and to guide the reader to see the elegance of the process more so than historically marking according to a solar calendar. In the prophetic tradition of the Hebrew Scripture, prophets would speak poetically about the "day of the Lord" when they were communicating God's creative intervention in the world, when injustice would be set right.

God's creative use of time seems to suggest that the "days of creation" or the "day of the Lord" are themselves a sort of focused transformative container. A shorthand, time-boxed way of knowing "what time it is." An indication of God's in-the-moment-ness instead of just a time stamp in an endless line of cause and effect relationships.

> God saw all that he had made,
> and here: it was exceedingly good!
> There was setting, there was dawning: the sixth day.
> (Genesis 1:31 FBM)

Scripture's creation accounts teach us that, not only did God make day and night, but God also paced the creative work into moments. If we learn anything about those moments, it is that God enjoyed being in the creative flow during each one of them. God saw something that looked "good," and must have felt some pleasure and satisfaction with it.

And then God intentionally time boxed a seventh of these moments for rest. We are told that God's time boxing was a sort of sanctifying, setting apart, or hallowing of that session, from the rising of the sun to its setting. Just as God marked the space under Moses' feet as holy, we see God sanctifying receptive, open rhythms into the creative process, a space for dreaming, hovering, listening, resting; naming this use of time as holy; devoting it to the calling to participate in God's work.

Our unlikely hero, Moses, wrestled against time during his encounter with God at the flaming shrub. When commissioned by God to fetch the people of Israel from Pharaoh, Moses is afraid about how that future would unfold. Will people believe him then? Will he have enough credibility at that critical moment? And so Moses asks for a credential to carry with him, the name of God, God's identity from all time. God's response becomes the name that Israel will know God by from that point forward, "I Am." Instead of fortune-telling who he will be or producing his birth certificate from ages past, God offers a name that is a literal snapshot of timelessness in the present.

God said to Moses, "I AM WHO I AM." God said further, "'Thus you shall say to the Israelites, "I AM has sent me to you."'" (Exodus 3:14 NRSV). The language can also be translated to read: "I am what I am," or, "I will be who I will be."

It's like one of those pictures of a moving mountain stream, when the water looks more like smoke because the shutter was left open long enough to capture the motion. God is telling Moses that God's name is "I Am Present"—whenever you happen to be inquiring, the answer is always God's presence, God's present-tense-ness.

Why all this talk about time? These metaphors suggest that God's creative work was not some line of cause-and-effect relationships, it was not the product of well-managed time, and it was not driven by an external purpose statement or deadline. Time (like space and matter) was handled with care, treasured, and breathed into life by the artistic intentions of God. Time is that vehicle in which "our soul finds its God and its home" as love "proceeds from us." And perhaps, since I Am put so much intention into our present, we'd do well to meet God in that same present moment.

Noticing This Moment within God's Art

exercise 15

If you can walk outside or to a private place to pray, take the next ten minutes to reorient your awareness of God's presence in the here and now. Have you found a place? Okay, now think about the next seven minutes. Set a timer on your phone or watch, and for those seven minutes "take every thought captive" and then dismiss it. Before you start the timer, read the following instructions: Visualize your thoughts, your plans, even your anxiety about this exercise as wind running across a still pond. Let each thought pass by and return to stillness. Imagine the Spirit of God who hovered over the waters of creation hovering over this moment. Be still and know that I Am is in your midst. When the alarm does goes off, slowly open your eyes and look around you. Then, return to your place to dig into your other work or the next chapter.

chapter 6

Working with Others

Returning to Mr. Dirt-n-Breath: the Creator intentionally places creation into a story where it can flourish.

In the first creation account we learn that humans are born into a world where the animals of the sky, land, and sea are already blessed to flourish. And yet, in spite of the flora and fauna being created all around it, Mr. Dirt-n-Breath's loneliness is palpable. God's creation of a time, space, and matter reality born from the vision of mutual self-transcending love is not quite right. Or, to use the language from earlier chapters, God's grand work of art, begun as dream, wants to moves into reality.

After taking the big risk of placing the human into the integrated grand work of art, God listens to it all, discovering what to do next.

The square-dancing, imagineering God determines that a group dance requires more partners and decides to makes a new being. Only this time, the being is part-and-parcel of Dirt-n-Breath. It is made from the rib of Adam. So then God's addition of interrelatedness changes the solitary humanoid into the human race, an interrelated species. We are all connected to each other from that first rib. And every human gets here through the power of connectedness—material things meeting up. Integration of egg and sperm is each and every person's beginning, from then on. And integration continues. Just as God is not solitary, humanity is communal and designed for interrelatedness. As Emmylou Harris sings, God is "in the blood of your heart / The breath of your lung" and we are "from the dirt of the earth / And the kiss of [God's] mouth."[35]

So the recipe for the human race is now part dirt, part breath of God, and part derivative of the other. We're all basically integrated stuff enlivened by God's lips and shaped by God's artistic use of time and space. We're all God's artwork, not just cranked out of an unconscious assembly line, not just add-water-and-stir. The very way that we are made implies that we are dynamic works of art changed by our engagement with created time, space, and matter.

When my wife and I were on our honeymoon in Victoria Island, British Columbia, we were walking around the town and came upon a glassblowing studio. We stood there for hours watching the process. The artisan would dip the blowing pipe into molten 220-degree glass, touch it carefully with various powdered pigments, and then rotate while blowing into the cool end until the object's shape set. Then she'd swing the pipe to draw the point into the orb until it came to a crest.

Blown glass is just sand under extreme heat and friction. Life's origins are much the same: dirt, God-breath, and friction. You and I are not alone; we are made from each other's pasts. The dust that is animated into who you are could have once been part of Moses or Napoleon, Lao Tzu or Joan of Arc, but in the furnace of this time and space and under the deft hand of God's present-tense creative touch, you and I become parents, musicians, neighbors. And what we leave behind will be breathed into again and again long after we are forgotten. "From dust you have come, and to dust you shall return." Religion resists the catch and release reality of change in this material world. But change is the very factor that allows for God's transformational artwork, as well as our commissioned artwork.

Change Is Movement in Relation to Time, Space, and Matter

In that glassblowing studio, the centripetal force of the spinning blowing pipe and the force of gravity are what pulls one piece of glass one way and another in a different way. The force of God's spirit, or breath, drawing us, expanding us, is what makes each of us unique. Change is responsible for novelty. Something novel or unprecedented, whether it be the uniqueness of each snowflake or the uniqueness of each artist's screen print is caused by the dynamic process of its creation. And so to live into those draws and blows, to be headed and flexed, is to be human. Change is a central part of what it means to be crafted or made. Plenty of other combinations of nitrogen, hydrogen, and carbon do not make proteins, and plenty of other proteins do not contain human DNA. Yet our protean DNA enables dirt and water to become human thanks to the very possibility of change.

Not only that, but change exerts its effect on us based on the DNA of the Imagineer. God created Mr. Dirt-n-Breath in God's image. Through the breath of God we have the DNA to become the actual people God has been waiting for. You are made with a dream in mind. The grand artist picks us up, like the blowing pipe dipped in molten glass, with an idea of what we can become. And the gravitational pull of God's dreams stretches us from the present into a promised future shape.

Imagine the ramification of God's gravitational pull while reading Paul's letter to Ephesus: "We are God's workmanship, created in Christ Jesus to do good works, which God prepared in advance for us to do" (Ephesians 2:10 NIV). Our relationship to the Creator, being dipped out of molten stuff by the blowing rod, is not what's under negotiation—it is already accomplished in and through the resurrecting power of Jesus. What is left undone, what remains to be seen, is *how* we as individuals and cultures belonging to this material world will be stretched and spun and blown into our intended shapes, refracting light in this moment of God's dreamed-for installation of a good-working world.

We are engineered with an imagined purpose. We were made with functionality in mind. In fact, your function is one of harmony—everything you make is a part of the bigger unfinished art project!

We are not just God's craft, we are also part of God's crafted realm: a realm teaming with interaction, a place and time anticipating the day of the Lord, when the Imagineer's dreams for a self-transcending, loving world is complete. We are created with our own collaborative creativity in mind.

exercise 16   *Noticing Change*

In this exercise you'll compare your current routine with your routines from seven years ago. Call up an old friend who knew you seven or more years ago. After catching up, ask him or her to briefly help you recreate your daily routine from those days. Think of when you would get up, where you would spend leisurely time, when you went to bed, the places you slept and showered, the food you ate, the rhythms of your week and year. After your conversation is over, write in your journal a description of that life seven years ago. Then, take some time to do the same with your current routines and rhythms. Compare the differences or surprising similarities. Biologists have found that our cells in our body change regularly. Some cells only live five days, while some tissue, such as those in the intestines, live an average of eleven years. So while you and I go on with everyday life, the very atoms that comprise us are traded out for new ones. What do you do with your cells today and how would you like them to function differently in the years to come?[36]

Working with Foreign Things

My friend, Holly, is a fine artist in Portland, Oregon. She's been working for years with photography, oil and acrylic paints, line drawing, and graphic design. Recently she took up the ancient medium of encaustic wax painting as well.

For years, oil and acrylics helped her best communicate what she was ready to express. But after the birth of her second son, she was settling into a new place with less and less time for creating and waning inspiration. She told me she picked this new wax medium out of a desire to say something new.

Encaustic paintings are made by introducing pure pigment to molten beeswax and damar resin. Painted on wood using heat, brushes, knives, and needles, the process moves quickly, much faster than oils and acrylics. The final product has a frosting-like finish that can hold layers, can be carved into, and can set apart colors in opaque and translucent ways. Working with something "foreign" from her usual disciplines, Holly is learning more about her process and discovering something new to demonstrate artistically about her current stage of life as a mother of two and small business owner who is entering middle age. When using oils, she said, "I got into a rut of repeating colors or patterns from prior works." This new medium is allowing her eyes to see more deeply into the moment and to reflect on the shaping hands of God's time, space, and matter in her life.

Too often, in life as well as in spirituality, we settle into a familiar subset of time, space, and matter, because we believe we've said all we need to. And why not? Maybe we assume God has completed creation, that the resin has set, and the colors are final.

And yet God's work of art has never stopped. In fact, it picked up momentum like never before in the resurrecting work of Jesus. We learn in the Hebrew Bible and the New Testament that God's art is expansive, from the beginning of time, when God crafted Eve and a subsequent race of humans as a revision of the solitary Adam; to God sending the Israelite spies home with Rahab the Canaanite prostitute to seek political sanctuary; to Ruth the Moabite being adopted into Boaz's family and becoming King David's grandmother. And Jesus carried on this vision when he interacted with the Samaritan woman at Jacob's Well. Philip continued the expansive tradition when he baptized the Ethiopian eunuch; Ananias, when he welcomed the church's archrival, Saul, into his home; and Peter, when he dared to step foot into the Gentile home of Cornelius, the imperial corrections officer who also feared God and cared for the poor in his town. God's grand work of art teaches us that without the *other*, without novelty, transformation does not take place, art cannot happen, and life's beauty fades into the mundane or burdensome.

Remember when we spoke in chapter 1 of the Trinity being a chord rung throughout time; an interpenetrating harmony of single notes, each setting the other off? This is where we begin to see that same love's role in our own identity as well. Thomas Merton wrote:

> We do not exist for ourselves alone, and it is only when we are fully convinced of this fact that we begin to love ourselves properly and thus also love others. What do I mean by loving ourselves properly? I mean, first of all, desiring to live, accepting life as a very great gift and a great good, not because of what it gives us, but because of what it enables us to give to others.[37]

God's love is regularly reintroduced to creation to shape it into God's dreams. That good-*working* world for which we are being designed (Ephesians 2:10) is an interrelated world. A good-working world implies cooperative fellowship between others.

Work is a relational concept. In physics, work is the combination of force and matter, and it either places matter into motion (moving relative to other matter) or it creates a molecular change. In much the same way, our function as "craft of God" imagineered to participate in the good-working world means that to understand our service to God is to understand our connection to everything else. It's as if God is creating all of creation to dance to the rhythm of love.

Why all this talk about *stuff*, *footprints*, and *moments*? Because without seeing that these parts of reality are where God exists in our midst, we stumble into an idea that God's plans for us are constrained to what is familiar. What is unfamiliar or other, then, becomes suspect or profane. In this perspective, familiar friends and families, our things, the traditional uses of space, our intellectual property, and typical segments of time are, supposedly, the only places where God exists, while other people, things, space, and times are not so. We limit our horizons and limit God to what we have already known or been told. And so we quit learning. We quit turning aside. We dismiss burning bushes. Instead we try to bottle our previous burning bush experiences, and in doing so, we miss our inheritance—a land where the Creator is still at work around every corner.

Mistaking *Our* Art for *the Artist*

If we fail to see that all time, space, and matter work for God's creative purposes in this way, then we begin to make certain times, certain spaces, and certain material things exclusively sacred. We helpfully see love become concrete, but then become beholden to the concrete thing itself instead of the encounter with God's creative realm through which all things move and have their being. In Judeo-Christian history preoccupation with making and protecting a concrete thing in and of itself has often been called idolatry. This is what Israel did after their escape from Pharaoh's army in their early days in the wilderness. When they saw God's provisions of gold from Egypt as signs of their redemption, the gifts themselves became precious to them.

Moses had left again to talk with God, because Israel was afraid to let God "speak to" them (Exodus 20:19). After several days with Moses away, they grew anxious and impatient. They fell into the old habit that their oppressors in Egypt had formed within them, the habit of restless production. As they had mixed brick after brick after brick in Egypt, now they melted down the gold stuff that once was a holy sign of their salvation and made it into a solid, static object, a golden calf, so that they could worship God. Meanwhile, Moses was on Mount Sinai getting crafting instructions from God. God instructed Moses in everything from building an Ark for hold God's words, to freeing their minds from Egypt's oppression through Sabbath habits. Notice how the poetry of God's instructions in chapter 31 (immediately before the building of the calf) reinforces the significance of freedom from restless production through the repetition of the word *make*:

> For six days is work to be made,
> but on the seventh day
> (is) Sabbath, Sabbath-Ceasing, holiness for YHWH,
> whoever makes work on the Sabbath day is to be put-
>   to-death
>   yes, death!
> The Children of Israel are to keep the Sabbath,
> to make the Sabbath-observance throughout their
>   generation
> as a covenant for the ages,
> for in six days
> YHWH made the heavens and the earth,
> But on the seventh day
> He ceased and paused-for-breath.
>   (Exodus 31:15–17 FBM)

God was clear that life of endless making would be no life at all.

When Israel sent Moses up the mountain to meet with the reality of God, they persuaded the priest, Aaron, to make for them the golden calf to substitute for the real in the meantime. We read in Exodus 20 that Aaron then instituted a festival for YHWH where the calf served as a seemingly innocent liturgical tool. This is how idols begin: as simple innocuous things. Similar to making a shortcut icon on your computer desktop, idols happen when we take a fluid moment and harden it so that it stays where we left it. But God does not always stay where we leave God. God is on the move, expanding, dreaming, creating.

Shortcuts, in and of themselves, are not the biggest problem; their harm is in how they are utilized. Remember the community organizing skill of Theory U moving groups from A to B through attentive steps of trust and courage? Idols are the opposite—they rush us to our own preferred point B. And then we insist that *our* tribal idols and customs trump other idols and customs. We argue over whose truths or whose practices are superior and end up reversing that presencing practice.

This happened to Jesus and his disciples as they walked along the countryside gathering grain from the fields or healing on the Sabbath. Their contemporaries, in a desire to defend the god of their precedent, would seek to discredit and eventually exact violence on those who refused to act like "man was made for the Sabbath."

To continue to live aware of God's crafting of *stuff*, *footprints*, and *moments* is an important antidote to making idols out of the familiar. They are also important as an antidote to avoidance. Time, space, and matter can force us to face God when we'd prefer to run and hide. If you'll recall from the last section, Israel, while wandering in the desert, was afraid of meeting God. The backstory is found in Exodus 20, when God invites Israel to a meeting at God's smoking, trembling mountain. They were terrified at such a prospect and they refused. To avoid an encounter of that magnitude, they ask Moses to be the middleman. Today we use more sophisticated tools to keep God above or out of reach from these realms. As harmful as creating gods out of our own time, space, and matter is, the habit of placing so-called godly things out of our reach is equally dangerous. Often we resort to putting certain elements just high enough in the kitchen cabinet that we need a stool to get there. Doing so keeps our encounters with God on a more occasional basis. To protect ourselves or our churches from failure or confrontation, we relegate the "things of God" to the realm of the invisible, intangible, and nontemporal.

Jesus, however, would spend much of his ministry walking among people and inviting them to discover that the kingdom of God is not out there somewhere, but "within you." The realm of God is as near as the seed is to the dirt, as integral as the yeast is to the bread, and as connected to us as the vine is to the grape.

Get Real!

I heard a lecture once where philosopher and Christian spiritual practice teacher Dallas Willard described the kingdom of God as "the reality of God's realm." He said that reality is the name we give to phenomena like running into a wall or pedaling a bike. Reality is a combination of something we learn and learnings handed down from what happens within our perceivable world. In this way, the realm of God's art is very real and experienceable from within this place, inside creation. Sometimes, the need to invent a god outside of the creative project is born out of an anxiety that we're losing a portion of time and space or matter that should be ours, free from God's dreams, free from the contributions of others. Other times we relegate God to the "outside" as a form of despair that the Creator has nothing more to do with the art project, perhaps the same despair that marked Moses' forty years as a sheep herder in Midian.

Remember when we described the potter listening to the clay as it unfolded into her hands? God envisioned the possibility of Mr. Dirt-n-Breath as God scooped him into God's hands. God saw the significance of the environment when selecting where the human would be planted. And God saw the significance of the present, when God self-identified to Moses as "*Here* I Am," instead of "There I Was," or "There I Will Be."

Painter and sculptor Michelangelo has been quoted to say this about seeing: "In every block of marble I see a statue as plain as though it stood before me, shaped and perfect in attitude and action. I have only to hew away the rough walls that imprison the lovely apparition to reveal it to the other eyes as mine see it."[38] In a like manner, Jesus' eyes were attuned to see the statuesque beauty within the time, space, and matter around him. And when he saw it, he knew it was the material of new creation. He did not dismiss the Samaritan woman as other; neither did he allow the laws about Sabbath to keep his healing touch out of reach from the here and now.

When God creates, everything is at God's disposal. And you and I and the others around us are being drawn into God's work of art through everyday moments, through our modest footprints, and through the stuff that we come from and encounter. As we'll discover in the second section of this book, we actually get drawn in to God's artwork through the act of making art. When we shape these same things into demonstrations of God's dreams, we more deeply encounter God and God's realm. But for now, be created. Make Sabbath and retrain your mind to see God in everything, to see the realm of God through time, space, and matter, to enjoy learning by encountering the other. Enjoy dreaming and resting with the concept that everything, since the moment God breathed it into existence, is pregnant with possibility!

...Earth's crammed with heaven,
And every common bush afire with God:
But only he who sees, takes off his shoes,
The rest sit round it, and pluck blackberries,
And daub their natural faces unaware
More and more, from the first similitude.
—Elizabeth Barrett Browning, 1857[39]

Noticing the Change in What You Regard as Holy

exercise 17

Review the ways that stuff, space, and time play a role in your life. Which songs, places, books, or moments have helped you recognize the creative presence of God? Which have worked to prevent you from recognizing or acknowledging God's nearness? Which ones did you hold as sacred earlier in your life, but no longer find meaning in today? And what things did you earlier write off as mundane or profane and now view as holy? Take a deep breath and thank God for *all* of these things.

Following Our Senses into God's Material World

I once served as a manager of a small community coffee shop where I met some extraordinary people.

One afternoon a man came in; he had a round, bearded face, beige skin tone, curly hair, and was wearing a pale yellow short-sleeved button-down shirt and a large polyester tie. Picking up various books we had on hand, he chattered on and on about them while questioning me about the neighborhood and the coffee selections. When he came upon one large coffee-table book about a primitive art exhibit featuring the work of the Gee's Bend, Alabama, quilters, he asked, "What do you make of this kind of art?" Without waiting for a reply he continued, "These quilters aren't trained. They aren't knowledgeable about the finer qualities of fashion seamstresses or textile art!" He sidled up to the bar with the book opened, and as we paged through together, he pointed out the inconsistencies and errors in their work.

As I discovered, these quilters were from a small, rural town surrounded on three sides by the Alabama River. The community of women there would stitch quilts for Sears Roebuck and save the scraps to build their own designs. To those scraps they added old blue jeans and whatever other tattered materials they could get their hands on. The result was a sort of jazz-quilting expression similar in design to Amish folk art and modern art.

The surprising fact to art critics is that these women had lived in poverty and obscurity while developing these same patterns without *any* exposure to other art as a reference. These women had artistic eyes as a result of expression, not through any formal education. They built these quilts after work hours as expressions of their own creativity, and they shared them with family members as birthday or wedding presents. Given their rise in popularity in the last decade, some of these quilts have been recovered from attics, cellars, and beneath the beds of the poor residents in Gee's Bend.

From the interviews in the book it would appear that the women of Gee's Bend made art for the sheer delight of it! They did it as a way of adding expression to their family's need for warmth. They never dreamed that the works of their hands would hang in galleries around the nation and the wider world.

As it turned out, the guy that came into my coffee shop, Bill Arnett, knew these women because he had helped write the book and to organize their national exhibition tour. He was giving me a hard time. He is an outsider art collector who has watched the rising notoriety of these women and their art, in part, because of his own craft in publication and promotion. And he sort of missed the hidden quality of their story before they rose to fame.

In modern-day religion we've also seen the jazz quilts of our faith hung in galleries. From unlikely heroes in Scripture to the founders' legends of various denominations or megachurches, we place certain stories on a pedestal and others under the bed. And as such stories gather time, we begin to evaluate our creative lives of faith from the vantage point of museums and ivory tower credentials. In the same way a trained fine artist might dismiss folk or "outsider" art, we dismiss the stories of our lives in search of pedestals and credibility. We are afraid to pick up a pen and draw, so we miss the chance to discover more about how we see the world. But these women created for the joy of it, not as an act of credibility. Art and beauty was, for them, a matter of play, not applied history or rational study. Living into the unexplored styles and possibilities made their art appear. They saw something in their minds' eyes and then they saw it through to the end. They took risks in design because they had nothing to lose. What if the shared life of faith were that much fun? What is it that we fear we will lose if we follow the artist's eye?

Seeing Is Believing

The familiar phrase "Seeing is believing" was coined centuries ago to note how our perception both determines and interrupts our systems of belief. The phrase has existed across cultures for centuries. The author of Hebrews wrote about the same correlation, but in reverse: "Faith is the substance of things hoped for, the evidence of things not seen" (Hebrews 11:1 KJV). This argument is substantiated by a catalogue of testimonies— real-life examples of those who rightly enacted faith. Just as my friend Todd would say that "love is concrete," the author of Hebrews insists that "faith is concrete"—it brings invisible hope and vision into sight.

Jesus' brother, James, would write about this as well, when he argued that faith has no shelf life, it cannot be kept alive through artificial preservatives. Citing the examples of both Abraham the patriarch and Rahab the prostitute, James wrote, "You see that faith was active along with [their] works, and faith was brought to completion by the works" (James 2:22 NRSV).

Faith moves from mission statement to action item. Faith is substantive; it is manifest in time, space, and matter. Faith operates in the real world as evidence of what is not perceived. Faith is not a concept, not an idea of something beautiful, but the realization or the outward evidence of the beautiful. In this way, faith is much like art. It moves the vision into the real lived space. In this chapter we'll be exploring the way that faith, like art, necessarily requires trusting and risking.

Art suspends time and space by putting us into the present as an active interpreter. "Millions of people can draw. Art is whether or not there is a scream in him waiting to get out in a special way," says the fictitious gallery owner and friend of the young Asher Lev.[40] I remember viewing the Gee's Bend quilts for the first time in the Corcoran Museum in Washington, DC, in 2005. They pulled me into the lives of these women, and then into my own life. Good artists do this by putting the viewer into play. God's grand work of creation does the same thing, "the heavens declare your handiwork," "the rocks will cry out," "the trees will clap . . ." when creation reaches its intended potential. Picture the great Imagineer brainstorming what kind of art will result in everything joining in chorus.

Worship works much like art: it awakes us to the *present* by putting us into play. And like art, if left to a conversation around ideas, worship cannot serve its roll of affecting people.

I often lead groups in Ignatian Prayer (see exercise 12) during worship gatherings, inviting people to engage a story or reading through their five senses. For example, in the story of Noah they might see blues and greens of water, smell the stench of dead things, hear the sounds of thunder. When I ask what people feel, meaning tactile or touch, many participants will unknowingly slide into emotions or similes that refer to emotions saying that the character Noah would "feel like he lost his house" or "feel afraid." And when a group begins to discuss and explore those feelings of Noah, they begin to identify with feelings they've had or currently have. The process of engaging the senses begins to root the participant sensually in their present-tense place, bringing the story to bear like a memory might in a therapy session, or the way a movie brings you to tears. As such, seeing is not the only form of believing; hearing, tasting, smelling, and feeling are as well.

Imagine with me the voice of God, calling. What does that voice sound like, feel like, what smells and tastes come to mind? The Word of God is living and active. We can taste and see the Lord's goodness. Consider the voice of God as more than a disembodied message. Imagine God calling Noah and his family, calling the young wealthy prince, Abraham, calling two brothers from a fishing village; in each story, the response to the call in the real world is what woke these people out of their under-inspired lives.

Noah, we are told, was an exception in a time of creative disaster in the Creator's world. Like the emerging artists who make something remarkable but return to the studio frustrated at the next wave, the Lord was "sorry that he had made humankind on the earth, and it grieved him to his heart. So the LORD said, 'I will blot out from the earth the human beings I have created—people together with animals and creeping things and birds of the air, for I am sorry that I have made them'" (Genesis 6:6–7 NRSV).

Imagine if God's approach to the creative project were to back off in the face of resistance. Imagine the temptation to hopelessness on the part of God's interrelationship: "This world has been a mistake. I've created a monster!" And yet God's "resolve to create conquers his regret" over creation's wickedness and God responds with patience and commissioning.[41] Like God calling Adam to name the animals, God's voice came to Noah and described the innovation that would come next: an annihilation of the violence that the creative project had made of itself, and a commission for Noah to be more involved as curate in God's grand creative project.

God proceeds to give Noah a supply list and blueprints, then casts a vision for what the completed event will feel like:

> "I will establish my covenant with you; and you shall come into the ark, you, your sons, your wife, and your sons' wives with you. And of every living thing, of all flesh, you shall bring two of every kind into the ark, to keep them alive with you; they shall be male and female. Of the birds according to their kinds, and of the animals according to their kinds, of every creeping thing of the ground according to its kind, two of every kind shall

come in to you, to keep them alive. Also take with you every kind of food that is eaten, and store it up; and it shall serve as food for you and for them'" (Genesis 6:18–21 NRSV)

With more clarity than ever before in the biblical story, an artist commissioned by the Creator is given responsibility for material means of rescuing and preserving future life.

In response to art that has turned destructively in on itself, the Creator intentionally connects the human's creative interaction with time, space, and matter to the future of God's creative enterprise. God builds an interdependent relationship between the mediums of the gopher wood, the craft of wood turning, principals of design and architecture, and God's unfolding plans. God roots the art in its relationship to an expansive future. Not only that, but Noah's identity will now be forever defined by that hoped-for future vision. God commissions him and his family to expand God's creation:

"Prosper! Reproduce! Fill the Earth! Every living creature—birds, animals, fish—will fall under your spell. . . . You're responsible for them. All living creatures are yours for food; just as I gave you the plants, now I give you everything else." (Genesis 9:1–3 MSG)

Take Abraham as another example. The father of Islam and Judaism and hero of the Christian faith is called to a life of intention that would shape the future. Here is God's commission of Abraham and Sarah:

The Lord said to Abraham, "Go from your country and your kindred and your father's house to the land that I will show you. I will make of you a great nation, and I will bless you, and make your name great, so that you will be a blessing. I will bless those who bless you, and the one who curses you I will curse; and in you all the families of the earth shall be blessed." (Genesis 12:1–3 NRSV)

While the vision God gave Abraham for leaving might have gotten him moving, it was Abraham's physical action (and not a disembodied vision) that would further develop the story of God. It was Abraham's art (acting upon time, space, and matter) that would further God's art. Centuries later, the apostle Paul would point out how calling and craft were interrelated in Abraham's life, "If Abraham, by what he did for God, got God to approve him, he could certainly have taken credit for it. But the story we're given is a God-story, not an Abraham-story. What we read in Scripture is, 'Abraham entered into what God was doing for him, and that was the turning point. He trusted God to set him right instead of trying to be right on his own.'" (Romans 4:2–3 MSG). Paul emphasizes the voice of God in Abraham's calling.

Like Noah's century-long construction project, and like Moses' dialogue at the burning bush, Abraham's engagement with God was not an intellectual negotiation about a detached divine plan, but rather about the strategic purpose of creation's relationship with God's creative design. Abraham entered into the artwork, picked up the brush, took his here and now seriously, and followed the vision God had given him.

God's callings to Noah and to Abraham and Sarah were more than instrumental means to ends. These people and countless others were drawn into play to discover their vocation by listening to God's voice and acting. As when the voice of God walked with Adam in the garden, so the voice of God continues to shape lives across time by walking with us. Parker Palmer writes, "Discovering vocation does not mean scrambling toward some prize just beyond my reach but accepting the treasure of true self I already possess. Vocation does not come from a voice 'out there' calling me to be something I am not. It comes from a voice 'in here' calling me to be the person I was born to be, to fulfill the original selfhood given me at birth by God."[42]

Like the jazz quilts of Gee's Bend, Abraham and Noah's crafts moved from obscurity to renown as they became inspiringly beautiful. Like the sound of a tree falling in a forest depends upon the eardrums of someone there to hear it, so the callings of our patriarchs and matriarchs were interconnected with their surroundings, and ours, insofar as they had the courage to act. Courage, his capacity to "hear," is what placed Abraham inside the script with God.

God is always working out the creative vision of a loving, interrelated world by handing off more of the vision of its cultivation to apprentices—people and communities brought into play by "hearing." Paul points out that, like the fish leaping out of the sea at the beckoning of God's voice, Abraham's answer to God's call was the very thing that placed him squarely within God's apprenticeship program. Over more than five centuries, that story expanded from Abraham and Sarah to a nation of tribes who end up enslaved by Egypt's dehumanizing story of power.

With the help of Moses, Israel was physically relocated out of Egypt for a life of participation in God's story; for forty years their imaginations and intentionality were liberated while they wandered the desert as displaced people. However, when they were finally given a place, their version of the story remained too small, so outsiders like Ruth and Rahab and Naaman were introduced to expand our view of God's intention: "filling all the earth" as God said to Noah, and "being a blessing for all the nations" as God said to Sarah and Abraham.

Seeing Again, the Prophets' Magic Carpet

I sat on the porch with my friend Derek, a talented musician who only recently recognized his calling as a Jesus follower—as an adult. His outside perspective on church life and Christianity is refreshing. As we sipped bourbon, he shared with me the stress related to recapturing the ah-ha of that particular moment when he knew God was near, the conversions that set him out on the journey that would lead him to church and eventually to our friendship and collaboration in music.

For the first half of his life Derek had had little to no interest in God or a life with God. This all changed one night when several tornadoes set down in the densely populated downtown Atlanta neighborhood where he and his girlfriend lived. One picked the roof off of their apartment. He retraced that moment when "our possessions and other random things were flying around the room and we sat holding one another under the kitchen counter. Somehow," he continued, "I felt an overwhelming sense of stillness and thought, 'Oh, *this* is what death is like?' I felt loved and safe, and I felt that Something/Someone else was holding us." He shared all of this with a bittersweet sense of longing.

That event that had opened his mind to the presence of God—and set him out on a search for a faith community—seemed so much more palpable and sensual than his journey since. It seems that our senses make precedents out of our memories and we can get upside-down when we try to creatively re-create the earlier moments.

How is it that our senses get dulled? What do we do when that nag for inspiration reduces what Parker Palmer describes as the "voice in here" into yet another "voice out there"? This is the place of the prophetic in our world—the Bob Dylans and Woody Guthries of every age who pull that rug out from under our feet.

In spite of the people of Israel's encounters with God's calling Voice in their midst, the dynastic nation would forget their orienting stories and eventually became like Egypt, their earlier oppressor. The kings and queens of Israel and the splinter nation of Judah eventually co-opted the creative energy of the people into a shrinking story of safety and idolatry. So, Israel's imperial version of God's dreams would be destroyed by rival imperial systems. Between the time of David and the days of Jesus, the people who once lived collectively as those called to live out Abraham's callings had become a people dispersed across rival nations and had then been reshaped as a vassal state of a world power.

During that span between national formation and Diaspora, while in exile and dispersed across the Middle East, the prophets would begin to deconstruct the previous generations' malpractice. They would confront the forgotten arts of life within God's dreams. They would subvert the false claims of the nations and empires in which God's people were dispersed. Even later apocalyptic works like John's Revelation would be filled with mockeries of imposter empires written in the religious code of his Jewish readers. The prophets worked through poetry, an art intended to be read between the lines. As poets they would repeatedly reorient God's people to the vision, the imagined dreams of God reaching back to the beginning of creation.

The prophets, as poets, had a way to speak between the lines. Poet and painter Bill Knott describes poetry as "the magic / carpet / which you say / you want," but which only works for you when you "stand willing / to pull / that rug out / from under / your own / feet, daily."[43] Poetry requires a lot of the reader and the writer. The commitment required is a self-sacrificing willingness to see something new. If, say, a Syrian or Babylonian oppressor had found news of a rival kingdom written in everyday prosaic language, they would have tried to destroy the writing and to suppress or interrogate those carrying the news. So the writings were encoded in the form of poetry for those with knowledge of the old Hebraic allusions and with a willingness to be moved.

Another noteworthy American example of art's ability to carry codes is the Negro spiritual. The songs that slaves wrote while working on plantations were adaptations of the oppressor's religion to both empower freedom of the imagination and to physically help the hiding escaped slaves find the next place in the Underground Railroad. For example, while invoking the desire for Elijah's chariot to "swing low" and carry him home, African slaves in America were also singing code words about safer passages and dangerous traps. Because the master did not have ears to hear the liberationist language in his own Bible, the slaves were able to use it subversively to pull his own feet out from under him.

Writing a Prayer of Inspiration or Lament

exercise 18

Think about your own ah-ha experiences in life. Can you remember when you first recognized yourself coming alive or filled with inspiration? Were you playing a sport, an instrument, playing in the outdoors, using a camera, drawing, or speaking up in class? Look over your life since then and list three to five times when you were awakened to God's nearness. Now list three to five times when you were overworking, trying to will the impossible to happen. Have you or someone you trusted made mistakes in the past that turned out to be an important guide onto a new path or a different approach? With these two lists in mind, read Psalm 124, often called a psalm of reorientation. Notice the ah-ha moments that Israel celebrates after the fact, as they rehearse the ups and downs. Take their historical examples and replace them with some from your two lists.

It's worth noting that we don't always live in Psalm 124 situations. Often, the jury is still out and the rug has been pulled out and we don't know who we are, we aren't confident in God's creative abilities, or worse, we only see God as distant and unengaged. If you're in this place, you're not alone. In Psalms 7 and 137 you can see how Israel maps their story as unfinished, demanding God's creative intervention. Perhaps you'd rather use one of these and replace their historic examples with your own.

The Open-Handed Character of Art

Poetry can carry hidden messages, but it is never simply a secret code. Art is not always conscious; it is also image and vision driven. It deliberately pulls the own author's feet out from under her. The illusive and suggestive nature of a poem often leaves its author exposed. Poetry frequently does more than spell out the literal description of a scene, choosing instead to trade in images. The strength of many poems is the metaphor's ability to attach to the reader's own life. Poetry chooses to show instead of tell, thereby allowing misinterpretation. The multiple meanings of words, the options of being misunderstood, are increased. Such writing requires a kind of humility or openhandedness on the part of the artist. The instrument of imagery is double edged. Insofar as it can effectively disarm the reader's defenses, it takes down the defenses of the poet. Beauty emerges from art precisely at that place where it remains free to be interpreted and shared.

The early-twentieth-century poet Rainer Maria Rilke compares writing to painting, saying the artist cannot afford to become preoccupied with trying to communicate a hidden message because the insights would slip unknowingly into the driver seat and the original sense of discovery would turn into a vapid, disappearing, fairytale gold "which cannot remain gold because some small detail was not taken care of."[44] The artist has to avoid the pressure and temptation to "illustrate" a disembodied idea, and instead must discipline herself to remain openhanded, free, and in a humble posture of discovery.

The late John O'Donohue writes that "freedom is the ether where possibility lives." Imagination has to work beyond the edges of the expected. It is as if the zone just beyond the artifact or the story is where the imagination is busy at work connecting the dots. Like turning the other cheek, art offers opportunity for something new to emerge. Poetry intentionally leaves this zone open, handing it, like a gift, to the reader.

This openness of art is an example of its generosity. Like God's creative work, the emergence of beauty that artists curate can be an expression of love, a gift.

Author and writing instructor Lewis Hyde teaches that the secret to the gift is its continual donation.[45] Hyde explains with a story from the colonization of America: Before the European conquest, a custom existed between Native American tribes that were at peace with each other. Pipes would be traded between, say, the Lakota tribe to the Cherokee tribe. Later, when the Apaches met those Cherokees, they would expect the gift pipe to be passed on to them, and they would pass their own pipe to the Cherokees. This sort of "gift economy," as Hyde describes it, was a way of remembering and inspiring generosity. When a European colonist and a Native American entered into those early friendships, the tribesman naturally gave the white man a pipe. And even though the white man did not necessarily have his own pipe to offer in exchange, the gift was freely given. But the white man, who thought in terms of commerce and saw their relationship as exotic, would then take the pipe and place it in a trophy case or even send it back to Europe. Imagine the disdain when that tribal leader would return to the house and not see the gift alive, or when another tribal leader would come expecting to get a pipe in return, having heard that the white man was now part of the exchange. The reduction from *gift* to *ownership* hurt the relationship between these two peoples.

This commoditization of the gift is some of what occurred with the news of God's calling as it was passed from Abraham through liberation from Egypt to the conquest of Canaan to the establishment of the Davidian and Solomonic imperial powers. The good news was being taken out of free circulation and put into a transactional place. This is what happened centuries later as the church under Constantine grew in size and power from enemy of the state to the state religion. But eventually, beauty subverts that kind of transactional domestication. Like a good poem that uses the double-edged sword of a vulnerable writer and reader, beauty pulls the carpet out from under those who seek to trade God's vision or calling.

Speaking against oppression, poets inspire both oppressors and the oppressed with images of abundant life and freedom. Speaking against triumphalism, prophets put the good news of God's big vision back within dangerous reach of everyone![46] And so, across history and into today, whenever a new authorized power would rise, the dangerous imagery they used to get there would then be used against them. Israel's prophets placed their claims to God's vision over magic carpets that would keep them from benefitting exclusively from the power equated with that kingdom. The Spirit of God will "blow where it will" and our grasping for control only makes matters worse.

As my friend Derek and I rambled about the deep desire to recreate ah-ha moments in our life—watershed moments of conversion—we noticed that inspiration is also tied to control. We realized that, just as in the music we both love to create, there is an inverse relationship between inspiration and control in our faith lives. As we admitted the lengths we go to control the Spirit, we noticed the ironic similarity to that whirlwind of things flying around his apartment four years earlier. Suddenly the realization came that no effort of ours can re-create zeal— rather, the reverse is true. It's counterintuitive, but like poetry working subversively below our desires to control, our ah-ha moments come when we let go of the management.

How an Artist Develops Eyes to See

Author Annie Dillard teaches that the writing life is similar to chasing a bee in search of honey. The author waits for a bee, puts it in a jar, and then lets it go and watches where the little bugger flies. Then she walks to the last place she recalls seeing the bee and waits to find another. When she does, she puts it in a jar and readies herself to start the process again. She lets the bee free and repeats the process until she arrives at the hive, within which lies the honey.

It is the honey chasers, artists, and people of faith who must keep an eye focused on the horizon. This artist's archetype to see what is next is often confused with precognition. We see the creations of culturally astute artists such as Charles Dickens, Sergey Rachmaninoff, Tennessee Williams, Diego Rivera, Andy Warhol, John Lennon, and Jeff Buckley as the ability to see the future. We describe such artists as ahead of their time. This is often the same attribute assigned to prophets and the reason modern culture frequently confuses prophets with fortunetellers. For the job of the prophet and the artist is to change our posture—from repeating what we already know, to perceiving knowledge breaking through at the horizon. Prophets were not necessarily channeling secret news from the future, but with a vision for God's Grand Art they artfully juxtapose the present with the possible in order to direct the lives of God's commissioned artists.

The Hebrew poets would reinforce this skill through their various psalms admonishing worshipers to "set your eyes to the hills" for signs of their Lord, the "Maker of heaven and earth." An oppressed people in ancient times would keep an eye out for the first glimpse of armies or merchants appearing just across the hills. The horizon represented a place of longing for an Israel looking for the return of God and God's society of shalom. Jesus would teach this kind of future anticipation through his parables of the virgins keeping their lanterns trimmed and ready for a returning groom, and the farmers in the field being swept away unexpectedly. But one of the most poignant examples of anticipation from the life of Jesus occurs after his execution.

Word was spreading around Jerusalem that the dead-and-buried Jesus had been seen, but many of the disciples had not yet witnessed the resurrected Lord. They were disbanding from the three-year movement they'd been on following Jesus from town to town, learning about the dreams of God. One particular pair of disciples were on their way home down the seven-mile road from Jerusalem, on their way to Emmaus after witnessing the trial and execution of Jesus spending their Sabbath grieving over meals of the Jewish equivalent of lasagnas and casseroles. On that road home they met a stranger who asked about the current events. When they told the tragic news of Jesus' rigged trial and unjust execution, and the rumors of his resurrection, the stranger reinterpreted the familiar texts of Moses and the prophets. The stranger pulled the rug out from under their feet to demonstrate that they were not beyond the scope of God's vision, but living in the very midst of it.

Previously we described poets who juxtapose the present with future possibility; in this case the stranger was contrasting the memory or promises from their past to the news of the present. Similar to the prophet, the stranger walking to Emmaus created possibility through images, and the disciples' hearts were warmed, their courage was reignited. Once the stranger broke bread and the disciples recognized that he was Jesus, they reflected on the way the transformation took place: "Were not our hearts burning within us while he was talking to us on the road, while he was opening the scriptures to us?" (Luke 24:32 NRSV).

This story harkens to the psalmist describing God's Word that "walks ahead of us" like a lamp ahead of our feet—not as one detached from the past, but as one that we discover to be connected to the past through lived experience, by walking along with him. In the words of Zechariah, John the Baptist's father,

"God's Sunrise will break in upon us,
        Shining on those in the darkness,
    . . .
Then showing us the way, one foot at a time,
        down the path of peace." (Luke 1:78–79 MSG)

Learning from the path unfolding ahead of us is not conventional. As modern followers of Jesus we want such a sunrise to enlighten us further ahead than "one foot at a time." Otto Scharmer of Theory U has called this ability to learn anew "presencing." In studying innovators across many disciplines he discovered that they do not learn in the typical "download information" way that most education relies upon. Instead he suggests innovators learn from the future as it unfolds.[47] Like our beginning discussion of the process of creativity from hovering through to reintegrating and resting, Scharmer suggests that innovators take a journey through a process from observation, to rest, to rapid prototyping—real-life tests in what they have learned.

In other words, this field of learning from the future is not about predicting what will happen *next* but is a process of freeing ourselves from former constructs that block our learning. It's like being born anew, being continually converted. Innovators must employ a free mind, a free heart, and a free will in order to perceive, appreciate, and act on new information.

Philosopher Elaine Scarry makes a similar observation when it comes to beauty's way of teaching us. Imagine the artist sitting in front of a palm frond day after day, amazed at the symmetry, the unfolding form that a palm makes with light, scale, and line. Slowly the form influences the creative approach of the artist. In a similar way, the disciples on the road to Emmaus were pulled away from constructed images of Israel's history and current events and were given time to contemplate God's presence then and there. The lesson taught to them by that stranger on the road required them to let go of what their minds thought about the circumstances, to open their hearts to God's nearness, and to free their will to join the possible scenarios described. Jesus had not finished teaching, he needed to die and resurrect for such a lesson to be learned. Their discipleship was to be a lifelong journey of reorientation. Scarry argues that beauty teaches in this way, "This willingness to continually revise one's location in order to place oneself in the path of beauty is the basic impulse of education."[48]

In the *Brothers Karamazov*, Fyodor Dostoevsky writes, "Be not forgetful of prayer. Every time you pray, if your prayer is sincere, there will be new feeling and new meaning in it, which will give you fresh courage, and you will understand that prayer is an education."[49] Prayer, like the creative life, opens up the horizon and leads to personal adjustment. A life of God worship, like *presencing*, requires loving openness of mind, heart, and will.

At various times, we who love and worship—and sometimes work—in churches realize these lessons anew. For instance, in 1967, at a time of cultural discontinuity, in the rise of nuclear proliferation, civil rights disputes, and awareness of the global disparity of the Third World, many American churches were struck by the discontinuity between their story and current events. They recognized that they could not carry all the answers for the future in their previously downloaded information about the world. They returned to the image of the Emmaus way and confessed that disciples of Jesus do not always bring the gospel to the world, but sometimes must learn from the good news that emerges on the path unfolding ahead of them.

At the time, a group of churches from the reformed tradition crafted a confession saying, the church "bears and follows" the Word of God into the world.[50] This subtle Emmaus-shift away from the church as an exclusive one-way channel for the gospel toward pagan, secular worlds seems to anticipate insights from both Scharmer and Scarry's work. The Israelites called this repentance, to "turn" one's direction. Interestingly enough, the root for that kind of turning is also used to describe Moses' action on Mount Hebron, "turning aside" to see that the bush was burning but not consumed. It seems that getting drawn into the story of God requires something like presencing; it requires a sort of confession—an ebb and flow between curiosity and witness—moving past the voices of judgment, pride, cynicism, and fear in order to "continually revise one's location."

The vision to see another world, and the openhanded courage to share that vision without controlling its effects, are also very much the life of the artist. These are essential parts of the prophetic tradition; what my old professor Walter Brueggemann has called the "prophetic imagination":

> Prophetic practice . . . consists in the courage, freedom, and daring to see the world differently. . . .
> It is no wonder that such a capacity to "imagine" the world differently refuses dominant ideologies of state, church, and corporation that serve status quo vested interests and seeks always to expose and subvert such mis-truth that deceives and denies. It is for good reason that prophetic imaging is characteristically done in daring metaphor, surprising rhetoric, and scandalous utterance, for to do less is to fall back into conventional distortions of reality.
> Its task—neither conservative nor liberal—is to expose and critique the false ideologies of consumer militarism and to propose a better world of neighborly justice and mercy. . . . Such practice—rooted in old texts and memories—requires courage, freedom, and daring, nothing less than the work of voicing and enacting the world anew . . . according to the holiness of God.[51]

Poetry, Brueggemann writes, "breaks fixed conclusions and presses us always toward new, dangerous, imaginative possibilities. . . . This speech, entrusted to and practiced by the church, is an act of relentless hope; an argument against the ideological closing of life we unwittingly embrace." [52] The prophetic calling is to create openings through the defenses that seek to close down inspiration and reformation.

Jesus was born into this tradition, speaking subversively amid foreign occupation while also subverting religious claims to power. Jesus used the art of parables as similarly subversive devices. These stories of approximation would require a commitment from the listener and yet leave the story open for expansion. As my friend theologian Peter Rollins has provocatively written, "Parables subvert [our] desire to make faith simple and understandable."[53] Instead, allowing them to do their work in us, parables "will change our world—breaking it open to ever-new possibilities by refusing to be held by the categories that currently exist within that world."[54]

And so Jesus would say repeatedly to his audience, "Those with ears to hear, let them hear." To enter into such parables as the prodigal son or the good Samaritan, the listener had to be open to self-critique and the expansion of his or her understanding of the kingdom of God. Otherwise the stories were nonsense.

Artistic creativity uniquely transforms one thing into another. It introduces novelty to a relationship. It observes things for what *else* they are. As we've seen, from a somewhat negative perspective, creativity pulls the rug from under the feet of its creator through subversion—taking something away. But it can also do so positively, through inspiration—breathing into existence. Trevor Hart, director of the Institute for Theology, Imagination, and the Arts, explains:

> It is precisely this "added-value" dimension of artistic creativity, the fact that art characteristically renders back something *more* or *other* than is given in nature as raw material, which has attracted suspicion and approbation

from those concerned above all for truth and an appropriate relation of humans to the reality of the world in which we find ourselves.[55]

And so, whether to subvert or inspire, Jesus places stewardship of the dreams of God into the hands of his followers. He would not shirk from "suspicion and approbation." He would not allow his contemporaries to co-opt a future lion-lies-with-the-lamb peace without them also taking their own responsibility to carry the oppressors pack an extra mile. And neither did his parables or teachings allow the wealthy land-owning priest or the extorting tax collector to imagine an economics of abundance and sharing apart from their repentance and reformed economic practices (forgive us as we forgive those indebted to us). To those who had grown accustomed to waiting for a secret hero or some divinely sanctioned practices to bring back the dreams of God, Jesus showed up saying that God's vision was being materialized then and there, requiring their whole selves to enter into the gift of new life.

Who better than the Son of God to walk into his home synagogue as a young man and read the poetry of one of the prophets about his Spirit-anointed call to bring the dreams of God to pass in the then and there (Luke 4:20–22)? Jesus knew his calling was to announce good news for the poor, bring sight to the blind, proclaim freedom to the captives, and announce the year of the Lord's favor.

But then a turn in the narrative took place. Jesus commissioned his apprentices to do the same, to be the very salt, light, and yeast that makes God's dreams tangible then and there. Jesus didn't pass a disembodied awareness of the Creator's favor to others without also commissioning them to be practitioners of that same good news:

"The Father has given me all these things to do and say. This is a unique Father-Son operation, coming out

of Father and Son intimacies and knowledge. No one
knows the Son the way the Father does, nor the Father
the way the Son does. But I'm not keeping it to myself;
I'm ready to go over it line by line with anyone willing
to listen.

Are you tired? Worn out? Burned out on religion?
Come to me. Get away with me and you'll recover your
life. I'll show you how to take a real rest. Walk with
me and work with me—watch how I do it. Learn the
unforced rhythms of grace. I won't lay anything heavy
or ill-fitting on you. Keep company with me and you'll
learn to live freely and lightly." (Matthew 11:27–30 MSG)

Just like other rabbis or traveling teachers, Jesus began
his journey by collecting a group of apprentices, or devoted
followers. When Peter and Andrew were asked to drop their nets
and become fishers of men, it was not viewed as an internship
or a telecommuting job. Their whole lives that had once been
oriented around trawling—keeping boats and nets, reading
tides, trade winds, and undercurrents, knowing spawning and
feeding cycles—these lives would now be oriented around the
cultivation of humanity. At first they would walk and work with
Jesus, witnessing the resurrection of the dead, the forgiveness of
sins, and the healing of leapers, paraplegics, and blind people.
But before long they themselves would be sent to raise the dead,
give sight to the blind, and cast out demons. And then they
would watch the mission expand as Jesus sent them to lead
seventy-two more people to do the same and to announce what
he had announced in that synagogue only a few years earlier,
"The kingdom of God has come near to you" (Luke 10:9 NIV).
Entering into what God is doing with creative intent is what
wakes us up to God's presence; it is the physical evidence of an
unseen vision.

Like the folk textile artists in Gee's Bend, the disciples' eyes
are developed by an inner voice waiting to get out and by

encounters with the material, not by critical study at an arm's length, or by downloading precedents from the past.

Jesus would continue to commission people to proclaim, to go, to do likewise, to create the dreams of God's heaven in the present. In accounts with Peter both before and after his resurrection, Jesus would say, "Whatever you bind on earth will be bound in heaven, and whatever you loose on earth will be loosed in heaven" (Matthew 16:19, 18:18 NIV). And in the upper room after his resurrection Jesus would compare his sent-ness to the sent character of the men and women gathered there (and note the *hovering* Spirit):

> Jesus said to them again, "Peace be with you. As the Father has sent me, so I send you." When he had said this, he breathed on them and said to them, "Receive the Holy Spirit. If you forgive the sins of any, they are forgiven them; if you retain the sins of any, they are retained." (John 20:21–23 NRSV)

Just as Noah's actions would affect the future of the earth and Abraham and Sarah's practices would shape the future of all families, so the healing and forgiving work of Jesus' apprentices was empowered by that same Spirit to shape the material future of God's kingdom.

Seeing is believing. Those with ears to hear and eyes to see would enter into what God was doing. Those glimpsing God's vision from the corner of their eyes and taking the courage to leap are the commissioned artisans of God's vision. And those commissioned are called as well to leave crumbs for others to spot. The song of God is expansive. It includes the outsider. It leads the powerless to places of freedom while pulling the rug from under those who want to control imagination and creativity. God's creative work of art draws you and me into play by giving us the crayon to draw that very story.

Rehearsing Your Intention for Eyes to See

exercise 19

Look back at the passages of Matthew 11:27–30 and John 20:21–23. Pick a word or phrase that speaks to you about being created or creating. Repeat that phrase and then write it down..It should be short. Then take that phrase and add it as a reminder to rehearse throughout your daily routine. If you use an online calendar or a smart phone, add that phrase as the subject and set it as a daily repeating event at three times in your day. For example, last year I was reminded by my iPhone at 9:00, 12:00, and 3:30 to live "like a tree planted by streams of water, bearing fruit in season" (Psalm 1). If you do not use phones/calendars for reminders, use another method to create regular interruptions in your day-to-day routine: Take three index cards and write the phrase on each. Tape these cards to places you visit frequently, such as the inside of a kitchen cupboard, on your car's dashboard, or by your toothbrush. In either case, agree with yourself to take a huge breath and smile at yourself when these lines interrupt and rescript your day.

Meister Eckhart, a sixteenth-century Christian monastic and teacher, once wrote that "the eye with which I see God is the same with which God sees me." Enjoy contemplation and interruptive awareness as an exercise in seeing through God's eye and enlarging your own in the process.

OUR RELATIONSHIP WITH CREATION
(BEING GOD'S COMMISSIONED ARTISTS)

chapter 8

Incarnation: Where Work and Vision Meet

In the last chapter we spoke about the eyes and ears to see and hear God's art. While doing so, we made a subtle turn. You probably noticed it.

The first section of the book was specifically about *God's work*. But in the last chapter of that first section we introduced the turn of the prophetic tradition: *our own work* in God's creative way. Like a character jumping off the page into real life, we've moved from our identity as God's works of art to our identity as God's commissioned artists, from the subjective to objective.

Actors appreciate the nuanced difference between following a script and entering into it. In 2009, Bill Cosby was awarded the Mark Twain Prize for American Humor. During the Kennedy Center event, Malcolm-Jamal Warner, who played Theo on the eight-year running *Cosby Show*, told of the acting advice given him at his first meeting with Cosby. At the casting auditions, thirteen-year-old Warner read the script with the expected expression of the bratty kid that he had seen on so many previous family sitcoms. He said everyone in the room was loving him—everyone except Cosby. He recounted the following conversation: "[Cosby] looks at me and he says, 'Now, let me ask you a question. Would you really talk to your father like that?' Cosby said, 'Well, I don't want to see that on this show. I want you to go out there and work on it again. And you come back in not like a TV kid.'" Warner said that Cosby then gave him a great piece of advice: "Don't play the moment. Find the honesty in the moment."[56]

The difference between finding the honesty in the moment and watching or repeating the moment is the difference between getting into God's art and remaining an outside observer of it. Theologian Nicholas Lash has written, "Might it be that, in the performance of this great work of art [the scriptures] . . . self-discovery and the discovery of fresh meaning in the text converge? Might it be that the 'greatness' of the text lies in its inexhaustible capacity to express, to dramatize, fundamental features of the human drama?"[57] This capacity for the dreams of God as depicted in Scripture to bring us further into the moment and to then teach us more about those dreams is what actors and artists understand about the relationship between the subjective and objective.

Theologian and artist Nancy Chinn writes:

> We know God within the context . . . of ongoing creation, a process that invites the artist and the church to evolve, develop, adapt, discard and invent. Making art is a process of letting go of expectations and living in relation to materials, living with confusion and an iconoclastic attitude toward assumptions everyone else seems to hold. . . . Such art-making is often marked by embracing the mystery, confusion, struggle, darkness and earthiness from which sprout joy, healing, the *ah ha!* moments of true discovery and all the creativity of the imagination.[58]

This dual characteristic of letting go of our control over material while living into our relationship with materials is significant because Christian theologies often use subjectivity or objectivity to defend against art that "subverts mis-truths" or "refuses to be held by existing categories."[59] Art, and prophetic art in particular, eventually pulls the rug out from under those who are preoccupied with protecting or preserving God's Art from an objectivist perspective. Reacting to the chaos of being flipped over and losing control over their magic carpets, they resist the very inspiration in their midst, meeting such art with "suspicion and approbation."[60] To their defense, this reaction is a distortion between subjectivity and objectivity—a confusion about their relationship to God's art. They are reacting to the moment and missing the honesty in the moment.

These assume that they are protectors of the art and not commissioned artists themselves. There are many ways of reacting to this fear. Some avoid their anxiety through busyness, like the bumper sticker that reads, "Jesus is coming, act busy!" Some starve the fresh vision to death through relentless planning. While others, like the fearful steward in Jesus' parable of the talents, bury their commission to evade the risk of subjecting their work to objective criticism. The confusion in all three of these examples (and perhaps others that may come to your mind) is over our relationship to both work and vision.

Jesus showed incredible integration between work and vision—being both the one through whom "all things came into being" and yet knit in his mother's womb as a human who did not "regard equality with God as something to be exploited" (John 1:3, Philippians 2:6 NRSV). Just as writing poetry from that magic carpet requires both the objectivity of putting words on paper and the subjectivity of allowing those words to undercut your intention, so Jesus amplified the interconnected relationship between the creator and creation. "He was in the world, and the world came into being through him; yet the world did not know him" (John 1:10 NRSV). Jesus stands among us as the first and foremost example of both creator and participant.

From the third to the fifth centuries, Christians debated the divinity and humanity of Jesus until most agreed that Jesus was completely both. As a council of church leaders from all over the Mediterranean, they wanted to avoid the two extremes of viewing Jesus as wholly other only "appearing" human or of Jesus simply being an enlightened human (popularized by a saying that "there was a time when the Son was not"). Instead, they wrote in what came to be called the Nicene Creed (because of where they met) that Jesus was "begotten, not made, being of one substance with the Father" as well as "incarnate and was made man."[61] Hart has written about this teaching that God's graciously placing "himself in our midst for touching, hearing and seeing means that this same 'physical' and historical manifestation must also be the place where we put ourselves in our repeated efforts to know [God] again and ever more fully."[62] We don't get to taste and see the nearness of God without creatively entering the human/material element!

You'll remember we began this book by pointing out that God did not exist as an example of complete independent isolation but as a relationship between Father, Son, and Spirit. We cannot talk about God from within the Judeo-Christian tradition without including interrelatedness. In a similar way Jesus cannot be talked about without including humanity.

The idea of incarnation, Word of God made flesh, is naturally impossible to get our arms around. And so it becomes incredibly problematic when we co-opt it to protect ourselves from creativity's magic carpet—from inspiration and calling. Some people want external authority for the status quo. We try to preserve Jesus' divinity by adding artificial preservatives of our own and pretending that Jesus never struggled as we do to create or forgive or love. We begin to believe that it's harder for us who are human to create God's work of art than it was for Jesus—in spite of Jesus' own words, that those following him will "do even greater things than" those he did (John 14:12 NIV).

On the other hand, in an attempt to find external authority for our creative freedom, we rationalize away the stories of Jesus' miracles and his resurrection as metaphors rather than unprecedented, God-in-our-midst experiences.

Jesus' way was a vulnerable one, like the artist, ceding power, and placing confidence in what remains at his horizons; remaining open to learning God's pleasure. Jesus is the deepest proof that God willingly stands on that magic carpet, ready for the rug to be pulled out. Jesus would say that it was not for him to know the end, only the Father (John 5, Matthew 24). In Jesus, we meet a creative God who is willing to suffer death (Philippians 2). "To recognize God in the crucified Christ," as theologian Jürgen Moltmann writes, is to recognize that "rejection is within God."[63] Jesus presents parables that narrow his audience to those who are ready and confound those who are not, further alienating himself and his neighbors. In Jesus, God took on damageable skin and learned loneliness, subjectivity, even abandonment.

In the same way, our calling—as human beings, as Christ-followers, and as artists—becomes real only when it is lived out in our vulnerable skin. We are God's work of art when we move into the honesty of the moment and "make art ourselves." We are not a secret menagerie collected by God; we are placed back into circulation. And as such, what God's commissioned artists create must also be a benefit to the rest of creation.

Dietrich Bonhoeffer, the German Lutheran anti-Nazi activist, once said that "the church is the church only when it exists for outsiders."[64] Elizabeth O'Connor, Christian author and early leader in the innovative inner-city ministry, Church of the Savior, wrote "we can never be in the world only as its benefactors. This does not make for authentic relationship. The covenant of the Church to call forth gifts is extended to the whole of humankind. I say to the world 'I will be an instrument of God in the continuing act of creation,' and the world fulfils in me its side of the covenant. It brings forth in me the new creation."[65] Just as the incarnate God has chosen not to exist independent of creation, no community of God's commissioned artists can exist apart from the audience for its work. Our work always involves what is outside of us and ahead of us. Like the Father, Son, and Spirit handing off to one another, our craft is about handoffs. Our hands-on work is handed to us in human, personal, fleshed out ways.

Apprenticeships: The Necessarily Physical Handoff of the Work and Vision

In the Bank of America building in Charlotte, North Carolina, are three large panels, frescos painted on plaster that make a triptych, an entangled abstract-realist story reflecting on making/building, chaos/creativity, and planning/knowledge. The artist, native North Carolinian Ben Long, employed a rare, modern-classical style that uses the dark monochrome grays we associate with baroque realists such as Rembrandt and Rubens.

A combat artist in Vietnam, he flew to Florence, Italy, on military leave where he fell in love with this classic form. Upon completing his tour of duty, Long returned to Florence to become an apprentice to the world-renown Italian artist Maestro Pietro Annigoni. Long's first job as an apprentice was making plaster casts; he then moved to grinding colors and eventually to painting-in panels that Annigoni had begun. After eight years moving from apprentice to journeyman, Long became a master painter with apprentices of his own. Eventually he matured to cocreating a fresco with Annigoni, as well as crafting the only non-Italian work of art in Italy's Abbey of Monte Cassino.

For one entire summer as a teenager in Charlotte I had the opportunity to visit that bank lobby week after week and watch those three twenty-three-feet high works of art unfold under the hands of Long and his student apprentices. I saw him initially sketching it on the wet plaster, I heard him instruct apprentices in the building of colors, the rubbing on of the gold filigree, and the application of layer after layer of paint colors and translucent oils that created his uniquely classic tone. No one would say that Long did not paint those paintings, and yet as many as eight people that I could see were working with him at any one time. Long used the formation work of the maestro-to-apprentice to extend his reach, his footprint. Long was a sort of conductor, bringing a sum of several accomplished artists into a greater whole. But Long did more than create an *artifact* through the orchestration of a host of apprentices and material; he also had a hand in creating those *apprentices*. He uses his paintings as chances to pass along what he had been taught: skill and vision.

Other apprentices in Italy at the same time as Long were American artists Daniel Graves and Charles Cecil. Together they were trying to bring the classical art forms of their mentors into their modern contexts. Graves later wrote a challenge to fellow master-artists to carry on this art of apprenticeship: "Amongst those of us working within this tradition, our knowledge and resources need to be shared, not only to further our understanding of our own work but also to better equip the next generation of artists to carry it into the future."[66] Graves, Cecil, and Long knew that as valuable as art is to the world, and as cherished as our insights and techniques are to ourselves, we must also hand those ideas and artifacts off for future generations to build upon.

What I watched those apprentices in Charlotte learn from Long, Long had learned from Annigoni, and Annigoni from his teacher. This is the artist seeing things through a long view, looking toward a larger end. While being single-minded, artists like Long teach others how to have that same single-mindedness.

Art functions best by gifting itself away as it draws other participants into the very creative process, and God's grand work of art is no different. As we traced the processes of God's lost arts of creativity, you may have noticed that God did not do these things only once in some linear fashion. Through the imagery of New Creation, Jesus taught how God's creative process is a regenerative one, continually part of God's character, and part of our calling as well. So far we've seen how the rhythms of God's works of design originate with loving dreams, a vision for what could be. Then God the Visionary, sits with the dreams for a while, hovering over their potential. After this time of hovering, God the Artist takes the big risk, diving into the moment putting matter into play. God the Risk-taker then takes time to listen—to be with creation as it unfolds, learning what else is next. God the Designer, watching for the nuanced needs and desires of the created realm, then places those created things in conversation with everything else, threading everything together like a jeweler stringing beads. Finally, God the Dreamer carves specific space for the act of dreaming, designing an intentional rhythm of rest and restoration for the apprentices who would follow. God's creative process continually unfolds with this end in sight: a creation that also continually deepens in relationship through creative engagement. God's work was always brought into focus in accordance with God's vision.

Our society loves leaders who draw people into larger end visions. Society is fascinated by visionaries in our world past and present, such as Dr. Martin Luther King Jr., Bill and Melinda Gates, Steve Jobs, the pioneering Stanley Kubrick, the enigmatic Andy Warhol, or Mark Zuckerberg—visionaries who "see things through" to an end. A visionary can take an idea and put it into action. We use ocular metaphors to describe these folks because they tend to offer insight into things that the rest of us don't seem to see. They utilize their mind's eye while the rest of us seem bound to our two eyes. Visionaries seem to have this extra sixth sense perspective that the rest of their contemporaries do not yet have the eyes to see.

Vision is a part of how our culture conceives of love and relationships. Various poets and lyricists demonstrate how the lover has "eyes" only for her beloved, that her gaze, her imagination, her intent is single-minded. The artisan, too, shares that single-minded vision of what she is crafting and, in doing so, sees that vision unfold, almost magically.

If you've known a person like this, or been in a deeply visionary period in your own life, you know how obsessed and engrossed a visionary or artist gets in their work. Andy Warhol was said to have demanded as many as three original recordings a day from Lou Reed. Henri Nouwen moved into a monastery for an entire year to learn the rigors of intentional life. Van Gogh cut his own ear off to demonstrate the passion he had for his beloved.

Society is both skeptical and aggrandizing of artist with vision to believe they've taken, in the words of Robert Frost, the road "less traveled by" when faced with divergent paths. The public figures we idolize say that their choice made "all the difference," because they chose not to remain still. People with vision choose their path and then walk with intention. This plays out every day with the pianist who practices diligently until she gets into music school, the family who saves carefully for vacation until it is a reality, the seminarian who takes ordination exams time after time after time until she finally completes the process. Writer Annie Dillard says that half of writing is "showing up." It would seem that artists show up long enough and often enough until they are able to will the nearly impossible thing into reality through their mind's eye. Visions that we've come to love can't be severed from the work involved in bringing them into reality.

We talk about the vision or the mind's eye of the artist because the sense of sight is one that notes depth and difference, on the lookout for danger or opportunity. That eye is a window into the heart, the place of imagination and purpose. Insight is seeing and discerning between reality and illusion. We say "seeing is believing" because we trust our sense of sight to most accurately define reality. And, it would seem, then, that the artists' knack is for introducing new things or a new construal of reality into the public line of sight. They magically make new things appear in public view.

The psychologist Carl Jung taught that "the dream writes the dreamer." Which, when stated another way, means that you become what you set your mind to. The opposite is also true: you seldom become something or make anything without seeing it first in your mind's eye. Whether you're planting a church, building a fence, buying a house, or painting a portrait, the visionary must see toward some sort of future possibility and make strategic and split-second decisions along the way according to that vision. Then, skills and labor, time, space, and matter join the process by integrating *vision* and *work*.

We've covered what that process looks like for many artists. And we've explored how time, space, and matter are animated through art into new renderings of what is real. Now let's dig more deeply into incarnation (Word made flesh) by investigating how vision and work operate separately and complimentarily. To do so we'll start with the relationship between work and vision in art's relationship to the viewer. Then we will return to the relationship between work and vision in the creation of artwork.

Work Is When Ideas Come to Life

Imagine you have an idea for a novel or a song or a play. You've been sitting on it for years. You decide you're going to get it done. You clear time in your schedule and you buy materials. You get all your notes together, and then it's time—time to make something happen. You look at the blank beginning, and you've got to just get moving. Ideas are a dime a dozen, because until you get them out of your head they do not "live." The work is what separates visionaries from daydreamers.

Thomas Edison famously wrote that invention is 1 percent inspiration and 99 percent perspiration. Creatives and visionaries know that visions die without dogged day-to-day work. Anne Lamott teaches writers to get started with "shitty first drafts." Julia Cameron teaches writers to wake up every day to "morning pages." And the real work comes through building on those disciplines with skill and the artist's vision until they produce artwork that stands freely as a new part of our world.

Interestingly, artwork offers the viewer a similar choice between work and vision. A viewer can walk into the gallery and see merely a painting with colors and symbols and texture.

The "mere" thing is an artifact made by a craftsman, no more or less, so to speak. The work demanded of that viewer in the gallery is to give symbolic meaning to the artifact and engage with it.

This way of encountering art for the viewer is a lot like the work the artist undertakes well. It deals with the purely physical and it gets very subjective and precise. Think of the most inspirational movies, songs, plays, or paintings that you have encountered. I'll bet that in every case the art offers you an opportunity to reconcile your own way of seeing the world with this novel artifact. In *Made to Stick*, brothers and coauthors Chip and Dan Heath teach about messaging and narrative from their respective fields of organizational behavior and business management. They suggest that various messages stick because they "break your guessing machine," the expected pattern of the viewer.[67] Art functions in this way, putting us in play as the viewer until, for a split second or for years to follow, our own vision is challenged by the vision presented to us in the artifact. Even in art that affronts us, *our* vision is provoked and brought back to the front of our own mind's eye.

The reverse is also true. The viewer who refuses to work rarely perceives what the artist is doing. That tender space between *viewing art* and *doing the work of seeing* is a place of trust. It is this intentionality that leads the viewer deeper and deeper into enjoying life. As in the exchanging of gifts or the give-and-take of relationships, art rewards hard work.

In both cases of the artisan and the viewer the two are related; they require one another. The artwork in the artist's mind is insufficient by itself; it must move beyond imagination and become realized through the process of hard work. And yet the beauty of an artifact remains under-realized if the viewer is not swept into vision and further insight.

Learning from the Trees

exercise 20

Psalm 1:1–3 reads:

> Happy are those
>
> . . .
>
> [whose] delight is in the law of the LORD,
> and on his law they meditate day and night.
> They are like trees
> planted by streams of water,
> which yield their fruit in its season,
> and their leaves do not wither.
> In all that they do, they prosper. (NRSV)

Notice that planted imagery. Now, take a walk and observe the trees around you. As you walk wait for a specific tree to draw you in. When that tree has your attention, stop and notice its roots. Imagine the aquifers flowing under your feet feeding the trunk and limbs of the tree. Notice the experiences of that tree held in the scars on its trunk. Notice the limbs reaching. Can you picture them "clapping their hands" as promised in Isaiah?

This exercise will help guide you in a meditation exploring what kind of tree you are becoming, but it bears some explanation. In the following passage from the book of Judges, Jotham, Gideon's last full-blooded Hebrew son, has recently escaped a mass genocide led by his older half-brother Abimelech. Jotham has climbed out on a cliff above a valley where Abimelech is being paid by clan leaders for the massacre of their sixty-nine other brothers. In an effort to expose the foolishness of their divide-and-conquer strategy, Jotham screams down at them with a parable with metaphors of growth, maturity, and the various vocations to which we are called:

The trees set out one day
    to anoint a king for themselves.
They said to Olive Tree,
    "Rule over us."
But Olive Tree told them,
    "Am I no longer good for making oil
That gives glory to gods and men,
    and to be demoted to waving over trees?"
The trees then said to Fig Tree,
    "You come and rule over us."
But Fig Tree said to them,
    "Am I no longer good for making sweets,
My mouthwatering sweet fruits,
    and to be demoted to waving over trees?"
The trees then said to Vine,
    "You come and rule over us."
But Vine said to them,
    "Am I no longer good for making wine,
Wine that cheers gods and men,
    and to be demoted to waving over trees?"
All the trees then said to Tumbleweed,
    "You come and reign over us."
But Tumbleweed said to the trees:
    "If you're serious about making me your king,
Come and find shelter in my shade.
    But if not, let fire shoot from Tumbleweed
    and burn down the cedars of Lebanon!" (Judges 9:8–15 MSG)

What various lives did Olive Tree, Fig Tree, and Grape Vine
lead? What would it have meant for them to give up their
self-responsibility in the rat race toward powerful roles as
trees waving over the others? What were the consequences
for the trees who surrendered their own self-responsibility to
the unrooted, dictatorial Tumbleweed?

Now think of your life. What is the oil, the sweets, or the wine that you are called to make? What are the aquifers that nourish you? What scars do you bear? What season is the most fruitful for you? Toward what do your limbs stretch?

When you have finished, take time to sketch an illustration of the sort of tree you are, or to journal about what you have discovered.

Vision Is Seeing What Is to Come

> *Just now, we squint to see the Image through*
> *this latent, bleak obscurity. One day, we'll see the Image—*
> *as Himself—gleaming from each face.*
> *Just now, I puzzle through a range*
> *of incoherencies; but one day,*
> *the scattered fragments will cohere.*
> *In all of this, both now and ever,*
> *faith and hope and love abide, these*
> *sacred three, but the greatest of these (you surely*
> *must have guessed) is love.*

—from "Love's Body," translation of 1 Corinthians 13 by Scott Cairns[68]

In the life of faith, *vision* does not necessarily mean we can tell the complete future any more than a painter knows what the exact painting will be before it is complete. Neither is our work arbitrary or random, any more than the craftsperson could build a dwelling by throwing sticks in the air. Faith, as in art, is about acting without completely seeing but still acting with intent. Indeed, to see our work through to the finish, we need to set our gaze on something.

In the above poem by Scott Cairns we can imagine the apostle Paul writing to the people in Corinth that their impetus toward good work along the path is not based in a total unobstructed vision of the end, but on a vision for love. In popular psychology today, some people call this work "visioning" or "visualization," describing the visionary's trained imagination. We already mentioned how God's imagination was born out of the self-transcending triune love that eventually leapt into the creation of the yet-to-be-formed heavens and earth.

Lucia Cappachione, a student of Buckminster Fuller who would become one of Disney's first Imagineers, describes visioning as "practical dreaming. . . . A method for finding the dream that lives in your heart and translating it into the world of three dimensions."[69] Each step of visual visioning, as she teaches it, involves moving from that dream into physical pursuits, such as collages, posters, paintings, songs, or dances until the dream becomes reality. Because a vision moves closer to reality when we can picture it, coaches and therapists encourage individuals to do the work of the artist, depicting their dreams as practice for the work of bringing their dreams to life.

But visioning can be much more than individual self-actualization. Physical artifacts that we can touch and see also help in communicating vision to a larger group. In marketing, Dan Roam teaches that "visual thinking [is] taking advantage of our innate ability to see—both with our eyes and our mind's eye—in order to discover ideas that are otherwise invisible, develop those ideas quickly and intuitively, and then share those ideas with other people in ways that they simply 'get.'"[70]

What if God also began this large work of art with the intent to have others "get" it? What if the greatest tool for teaching us this art, was to, in fact, move from visualization into the physicality of love and its possibilities, so that we might learn this kind of love? How, then, might we see differently God's promises with Noah, with Abraham and Sarah, and with Hagar, Ishamel, and others as steps in showing love—love that could be realized by those of us who "see" it? What does this mean for familiar passages such as, "God demonstrates his own love for us in this:

While we were still sinners, Christ died for us" (Romans 5:8 NIV). The word *demonstrate* implies that something is seen, taken in; it's that divine-human point of contact that incorporates both faith and grace.[71] Like a tree falling in a lonesome forest makes no "noise," the God who acts, must do so with others present. Like the artist who must freely gift the work for the participant to intentionally engage, it would seem that God's gift of God's son was one where humanity could engage fully, recipient and participant, for better and for worse.

A few years back at Neighbors Abbey, a church plant I co-facilitated, a conflict arose between two folks and had an effect on many of us. The effects were deepest on the spouses of the two in conflict. Eventually the two began to break through the tension and work toward reconciliation, and in doing so, they sought out ways to confess to others. When the wife of the one who felt attacked in the conflict offered forgiveness to the person who had offended her husband (and by extension, her), there was a shift in the community, a freedom, and a generative breakthrough. In the process of that confession and the forgiveness that the offended person offered, the offender grew into a deeper knowledge of God's love. She shared with the congregation the next week, "My experience of her forgiveness opened my heart to what God's love must be like. This friend, who has forgiven me, though I did not deserve it now serves as a memorial, a daily reminder to me of God's love." Forgiving love is not just a dream, it is a dream that, when put to the test, writes the dreamer. Forgiveness, like art, is vision translated into an artifact through real work, work that then deepens the vision. So when we pray, "Forgive us our trespasses, as we forgive those who trespass against us," we are asking God's dream to write us as dreamers, to shape us as artists of God's grand forgiving creation!

God, having a vision for a world where death is stripped of its power, bet on that vision in the ultimately selfless way, by entering into the physical artwork and allowing sabotage to run its worst course. Jürgen Moltmann writes, "In the way hidden in the cross, the triune God is already on the way toward becoming 'all in all,' and 'in him we live and move and have our being.' When he brings his history to completion (I Corinthians 15:28), his suffering will be transformed into joy, and thereby our suffering as well."[72]

God's love unites the dreamer. It is necessarily participatory. Witnessing the depth of compassion that would lead God to bear torture and capital punishment would teach—it would draw a community of love further into the story. Seeing the story then be reversed by introducing physical evidence of the complete vision—the resurrected body, the final product made present here and now—would compel a community forward to do the same. To enact God's love.

What could this mean for our reading of: "God's love was revealed among us in this way: God sent his only Son into the world so that we might live through him. In this is love, not that we loved God but that he loved us and sent his Son to be the atoning sacrifice for our sins. Beloved, since God loved us so much, we also ought to love one another. No one has ever seen God; if we love one another, God lives in us, and his love is perfected in us" (1 John 4:9–12 NRSV)? John suggests that our very capacity to see God is connected to the perfection of love within us. Or as Elaine Scarry put it, our "willingness to continually revise" our vantage point is fundamental to our understanding of that beauty. Our love for "God who we cannot see" is predicated on our love for others we can see. Not only that, but what if, in the same way that a work of art in a museum only grabs those willing to work, the life-changing effect of God's love only influences those willing to turn aside?

I'm not suggesting that work trumps vision, but that the two integrate with one another to complete creation in us. Tasting *and* seeing that the Lord is good is an integration of vision and work. Playing off of the book of James, late songwriter Rich Mullins once wrote, "Faith without works is like a song you can't sing." Perhaps the reverse is also true: Working faith is like singing a song. You hear it, you learn it, you join in, and you re-present it. In short, faith is singing ourselves into becoming God's song.

vision exercises

In chapter 1, we began to draw a connection between God's love and God's creative inspiration. Often the things we love can teach us a lot about our vision. What we find admirable or identify as glorious informs what we seek after. Choose one or more of the following exercises to explore this connection between love and vision:

Learning Vision's Connection to Love

exercise 21

Invite two or more people to dinner or coffee and try the following experiment. Begin the conversation with an exercise: *What is something that you really love?* You should go first. Once each member of the group has taken a turn, repeat the process for about seven minutes, offering up other things you each love. Encourage everyone to keep their answers short, with no need to defend or explain *why* this thing is beloved to them. Then just see what happens. Don't force anything spectacular; just enjoy it as a game. That evening or the next day take twenty minutes to journal or sketch on what you observed. Notice what your own awareness of love taught you about your vision or dream for your life.

Letting Vision Emerge from Morning Journals
exercise 22

Spend twenty minutes every day for seven days with a blank sheet of paper and pencil writing what comes to mind. Don't try to sneak in homework assignments or begin that long-dreamed-of novel; instead, use the place like a playground. At the end of the week read through and notice where love or anxiety show up. What does this tell you about your vision?

Letting Vision Emerge from Photo Journals
exercise 23

Take twenty minutes a day for seven days in silence to find one picture. Take your camera (or a smart phone with photo capabilities) on a walk outside or in your home. When something catches your eye, use your eyes to ask if it would be willing to be the subject of your picture. Wait and consider how it prefers to be photographed. For example, is that old water oak, or favorite hairbrush, or stray dog telling you how it wants to be photographed? Then gently situate yourself and take one shot. Don't edit it. Just return to your walk home. Once home, take a look at your photo and ask, "How is God's glory shining through this subject?" If you want to have some fun, put it on your favorite social media site, and hash tag #drawnin to include it with other people's photos and prayers.

The Dis-integration of Work and Vision

Churches have traditionally dealt with the relationship between work and vision in many ways. But as I've witnessed, some faith groups commit to naming the vision, while others commit to naming the work. Perhaps you've already wrestled with this difference through the course of his book. You might be blocked by a sort of chicken-and-egg dilemma, wondering "do I give up my dreams in order to work" or "must I stop working in order to dream?"

This classic dilemma for many spiritual artists that I know becomes a log-jam for creativity, blocking the artists from enjoying getting drawn in. As a simple test to see where you fall out on this, I'd like you to read the following quote and rate your reaction. Your response will likely prove which way you currently lean. Philosopher-theologian, James K. A. Smith writes about the tension between naming our vision and our work toward that vision when he says:

> "We can't not be lovers; we can't not be desiring some kingdom. The question is not whether we love but what we love. . . . Our love is always ultimately aimed at a *telos*, a picture of the good life that pulls us toward it, thus shaping our actions and behavior. . . . The way our love or desire gets aimed in specific directions is through practices that shape, mold, or direct our love."[73]

If you reacted against Smith's argument for a "picture of the good life" as a too explicit naming of the vision, I'll guess your faith is more committed to the *worker* side of the artist. Whereas if you were galvanized by a vision named as "a kingdom" that "pulls us toward it, thus shaping our actions," then I'd guess that you or your faith community is more focused on the *vision*. Granted, there are types of faith and types of churches that do not hit on either of these (in fact, I'm hopeful that the integrative approach in the following pages will encourage even more of this). But nearly every spiritual-creative I have met (and I'm no exception) can identify with the creative paralysis that creeps in when overly committed by a false choice to reject one of the other.

The Road to Nowhere

As a high school youth leader I used to take short backpacking excursions through parts of the Smoky Mountains. The park surrounds a large lake formed by the Fontana Dam built in the 1940s. On these hikes we'd often run into the Dam Kids, as they called themselves, men and women in their seventies at that point who had once lived in the towns now flooded by the damming of the Little Tennessee River. They told us that the flooding to build the dam had not only covered their homes but also cut them off from a cemetery where many of their parents and grantparents lay buried. Near the time of the completion of the dam the National Park Service agreed to build a new thirty-mile road through the mountains for these people to visit that cemetery, but the constructors were met with huge engineering challenges until the funds finally dried up and they abandoned the project. Today the road is only seven miles long and ends abruptly, so it has been affectionately nicknamed the "Road to Nowhere." People hike on it now because they enjoy the scenery, but there is no real destination at the end of the trail.

Many artists I know have felt the death of their spiritually creative energies lead to a form of *road to nowhere*. Some choose to exclusively emphasize the joy found in the work along the way, as if a long view blinds them to the present. Others minimize engagement with the work out of commitment to the envisioned destination, insisting that the destination is more postponed, out there somewhere, in an immaterial unreachable place of the divine. Each path has its appeal, and many of us have started down one until we just had to backtrack and jump over to the other because the description of the journey or the description of the destination did not match the experience we had along that path. So when worn-out by the journey or the destination, we settle for the alternate dead end of reactionism, rejecting one extreme for the other. The road to nowhere is a common writer's block, a useless compromise, like the half-finished road to the family cemeteries. Our previous discussion on incarnation applies here, because rejection of the path or the destination is similar to the rejection of divinity or humanity. It cleaves the inspiration from the material, the work from the beauty, the audience from the artifact. Either extreme leads to burnout and blocked creativity. The two require each other. In fact, the pull between the two is often the very longing and inspiration that fuels so much great art.

False Choices

Let us take a short look at these two false choices: rejection of the work or rejection of the vision. Some artists have, like Moses at the burning bush, experienced an inspiring calling to join God in this present time, space, and matter, only to meet a new friend along the way who says, "Come with me to a sacred place where, once you arrive, the burning bush never goes out." The problem is, this idyllic place usually comes with an agenda of some kind—membership in a weeknight dinner group, sitting through a certain sermon, buying a book or publishing series, voting for a certain party, giving to certain needs, sending your children to a particular school—all of these possibly helpful options seem legitimated by a claim that they are vision kind of people, but ultimately, they lead us to forget about our original intended journey. The beauty found in work is lost because craft is reduced to a simple means toward the agreed-upon end. The gap between vision and work becomes efficiently filled by loyalty to the destination.

Peter fell into a similar temptation at the Mount of Transfiguration. The spectacular moment of Jesus and Elijah and Moses in all their glory stopped Peter in his tracks. Naturally, he wanted the mountaintop experience to be definitive. The muse hit and he wanted to bottle the experience. He wanted to build booths, small chapels, for people to come and visit and be reminded of this moment. Luke reports:

> While [Peter] was babbling on like this, a light-radiant cloud enveloped them. As they found themselves buried in the cloud, they became deeply aware of God. Then there was a voice out of the cloud: "This is my Son, the Chosen! Listen to him."
>
> When the sound of the voice died away, they saw Jesus there alone. They were speechless. And they continued speechless, said not one thing to anyone during those days of what they had seen. (Luke 9:34–36 MSG)

But not everyone becomes speechless like Peter. Some feel compelled to more and more vision obsession, hiring and rewarding loyalty, and less and less craft beneficial to rest of the creation. Sooner or later such communities find themselves longing for a road out of here and shaping their church and faith life to answer such a prayer.

After so long of trying to live by loyalty to a finalized vision, many artists eventually double back or just run off the path toward the place of mystery. They begin to trust that "the only constant is change itself," an unpredictable future with no history of experiments and no vision of the future. Creatives do this because we intuitively know that creative living involves unknowns; rationalizing everything based on what we've seen once or hope to see again does not lead to free creative expression. Remember John O'Donohue's words, "Freedom is the ether where possibility lives." Well, that place of freedom, that gap between vision and work is the very thing that gets an artist up in the morning. Spelled-out vision heavy-handedness that attempts to minimize or bridge that gap caves under the innate desire to live a creative life—a desire that the Creator cultivates within all apprentices.

And so in reaction to the "road out of here," creatives might run to an alternative "final destination" cul-de-sac. Like Tennessee's road to nowhere, their journey ends arbitrarily, wherever the money ran out. People begin to stay where they are—numbed to dysfunctional systems, resigned to their victimization to various oppressions, having grown accustomed to the daily pressure to cook up something more inspiring than yesterday.

This second creative block emerges innocently, much like the first. Perhaps drowned in the mundane of work-work-work, artists might be surprised one day, just as Moses was by the burning bush that lay around the corner. They might discover that "God is found in the work" and commit themselves to their own road; they might drift from their familiar road and discover new life, as did the disciples along the road to Emmaus. They might see that they are being created in the open space of the journey. They might hear their calling to walk ahead into mystery. But as some travel, they grow afraid; they don't hear the names that they knew before. Others struggle to find patrons and struggle to sustain their work like they could along the path that repeated their vision over and over. Some of these journeyers refuse joining the prescribed political party or don't really want to attend the "right" schools. They worry that monetizing their art is "selling out." They collaborate less because these spiritual creatives don't easily reach agreed-upon long-term goals. They're great at thinking critically and originally about decisions in front of them, and yet that critical thinking gets exhausting. So they frequently change direction, jumping from dream to dream without integrating work with vision, in fear of naming that vision. Determined that there is no future vision pulling them, they fall into the immediacy trap of having to create their own momentum.

I've known artists like this who become alcoholics, who break up relationships, who run away from home. My own experience along this "having arrived" path is littered with false starts, unrealized partnerships, self-destructive habits, and half-baked art. These artists who emphasize work over vision are viewed as making things harder for themselves, but they are convinced that the difficulty keeps them hunting, changing, making. They avow to a life filled with "random acts of kindness" because intention seems too other-worldly or judgemental. Burnt out on verses of church that would leverage everything along the way to justify a destination, they give up on the notion of destination all together. Their pride prevents them from looking up for help, from finding themselves within a larger vision. They work and work and work only to find themselves back at the same creative block as the "road out of here" philosophy to which they are reacting.

The psalmist testifies to training his eyes on the hills as the locus of God's in-breaking help, because vision is crucial (Psalm 121). And yet, the hills are never the same. They resist flattening and propagandizing. Like the mystery of good poetry, we can't wrap our arms all the way around the hills. Each new moment that the light hits those hills reveals a new color or shadow or hue in the horizon. The horizon is constant and yet constantly changing. Each shift in wind, each travelling leaf or animal, each new arrival of travelers allows the community to reset their vision. There is a present place where the vision of "deep memory and exuberant hope" lies ahead at the horizon, as tenuous as the poet's magic carpet.[74] It is that mysterious inspirational place of longing. Perhaps the reason the Word-made-flesh did not always know the time set by the Father was so that he might truly know the bittersweet delight of the artist who watches to see what emerges.

This integrative way is a mixture of these two paths, a harmony of vision and work. The art of church, gathering as two or three in the Way of Jesus, includes vision, tradition, apprenticeship, and the daily risk of expressing this vision through the moments, footprints, and stuff of life. This is not a new idea. Many have walked the fine line between Moses' turning aside and Peter's transfiguration warning for centuries. As Franciscan priest Richard Rohr has written, "The human art form is in uniting fruitful activity with a contemplative stance— not one or the other, but always both at the same time."[75] The good work that God prepared for us in advance is one that is attentive to both the here and now as well as the Creator's envisioned destination for all things.

Integrating the Journey with the Destination

In Jesus' day Israel was an occupied territory of Rome. Much like our current polarized political environment, groups were siloed or pitted against one another according to their mutually exclusive visions: zealot revolutionaries, the Roman establishment, and religious sects that colluded with and subverted the empire in their own ways—to name a few. And Jesus was more of a "double belonger," a friend of people across these groups, associated with saints and sinners, a royal citizen of both heaven and earth.[76]

Some in the Jewish religious establishment believed that Israel's glory days would return through their arduous work and the technical execution of every last task prescribed in the Hebrew Scriptures. Other contemporaries of Jesus sought to work against their oppressors to stomp out bad visions through guerilla warfare. Their vision was also an exclusive one that sought to demolish their enemy's paths. These were visionaries, but their vision for a true restored Israel was for those who shared their path.

Jesus challenged this vision. Returning people to the earliest articulated dreams of God, Jesus' vision led to a path that involved caring for outsiders along the way. For example, he admonished his apprentices to turn the other cheek, to carry the Roman occupier's pack another mile farther than the law required, and to pray for their persecutors.

When various sect leaders would confront Jesus and try to catch him on a wrong work or wrong vision, Jesus would repeatedly utilize parables that would require his accusers to play along. Like the Pied Piper, Jesus drew his accusers into interpreting *his* stories, and in doing so, wooed some of them into apprenticeships in the creative way of God. He would say, let those with eyes to see, see, and those with ears to hear, hear. And it left people along divergent, temporary roads with a choice: turn aside like Moses while resisting making shrines out of transfiguration moments, or remain blind and deaf to what is happening right now. The incarnation event of Jesus was a confrontation, "Step onto the tenuous magic carpet or stay behind!" And the flesh-and-blood events of our lives as God's commissioned artists are meant to be the same!

Integrating Your Everyday Life with Your Creative Call   exercise 24

Nicholas Herman was a soldier in the Thirty Years' War, and then a footman before he chose to enter into monastic life and changed his name to Brother Lawrence of the Resurrection. His sayings are recorded in *The Practice of the Presence of God*. Brother Lawrence saw no difference between his time of business and his time of prayer. "In the noise and clatter of my kitchen," he would say, "while several persons are at the same time calling for different things, I possess God in as great tranquility as if I were upon my knees at the blessed sacrament."[77] He saw his destiny to be the present-day active practice of keeping his mind in God's "holy presence," and he felt at home the more he integrated this practice with his everyday life.

Take some time to recount the last twenty-four hours. List seven people you made life with—children, life partners, business partners, strangers. List the seven physical things that you built, washed, ate, threw away, or interacted with in some way. List seven choices that you said yes or no to. Can you see how each relationship, each artifact, each yes or no was an opportunity to enter the field of God's creative work? Take a moment and sketch or journal what it might mean to more deeply integrate your everyday and the places of inspiration in your life. Note where gratitude and desire relate in this integrative work.

Getting Drawn In

So how is it that we get drawn in? It is in being both artwork and artist, each teaching the other. We discover this as we put vision to work in a way similar to Paul's encouragement to the Galatians, "The only thing that counts is faith working through love" (Galatians 5:6 NRSV). We daily pick up the material world at our disposal and shape it, even as we're being shaped.

Our family loves the children's story *Harold and the Purple Crayon*. It begins like this:

> One evening, after thinking it over for some time,
> Harold decided to go for a walk in the moonlight.
> But there wasn't any moon,
> and Harold needed a moon for a walk in the moonlight.
> And he needed something to walk on.
> [Using his crayon], he made a long straight path so he wouldn't get lost
> and set off on his walk taking his big purple crayon with him.
> But he didn't seem to be getting anywhere on the long straight path
> So he left the path for a short cut across a field.
> And the moon went with him.[78]

The magic of Harold's story is the way the author wittingly leads the reader to recognize Harold's part in making his own reality. The plot thickens as you discover Harold is looking for something—his bedroom window. Along the way he imagines a forest with only one tree.

After a few strokes of his crayon, it turns out to be an apple tree. And so, to protect the apples that will soon be ripe and tasty, he imagines a fierce monster to guard the tree. The monster Harold draws is so scary that it ends up frightening Harold, and he falls into an ocean of his own making (due to the crayon held in his quivering hands), realizing in the nick of time that he can just as easily make a boat to keep himself afloat. Soon he makes shore. And (a long-and-brilliant-story-made-short) Harold eventually makes his way home by remembering that the bedroom window he so longed for belonged around the very moon that had been with him all along his journey. So with the moon, at last, where it belonged, Harold finally makes his bed and draws up his covers.

Harold's inventor, Crockett Johnson, does a brilliant job of playfully exhibiting how Harold's visions play a role in rendering his reality. Perhaps this is how we are drawn into God's own vision. The author and finisher of our faith does not simply hand us crayons; the Creator continues to create alongside of us in a master-apprentice relationship. We are works of God. Like crayons, we are intended to render a world. And we are also commissioned artists, like Harold, given the world as our art media. Perhaps we develop eyes to see what God intends in-and-through the very work of love intended by God.

All too often we imagine God as making things out of necessity. Not in the mother-of-invention kind of necessity, but as the obligatory strategic execution of a linear master plan kind of necessity. What recent studies in creativity teach us, however, is that most art, beauty, and innovation that we come to appreciate emerge from process that regularly return to play and empathy. The visionary is not engrossed in the project simply out of a workaholic pathology or outcome-based obsession. The visionary is engrossed because of the pleasure found in creating. The visionary is not detached and outside of the puzzle. Artists develop an affection toward their creations, a certain self-clarifying relationship with what is made.

Apply this science to God's creative exploits. God loved making everything we see. As each new creative exploit unfolds, it is bookended with the Hebrew poetic stanza, "And God saw that it was good." And God loves the surprise and beauty of the continued project as it is unfolding. Recent research teaches us that pattern recognition, puzzle solving, and manipulation of mediums are all connected to the pleasure centers of the mind. Popular author and documenter of the rise of the creative culture Daniel Pink writes, "Like its five siblings, Play is emerging from the shadows of frivolousness and assuming a place in the spotlight. *Homo ludens* (Man the Player) is proving to be as effective as *Homo sapiens* (Man the Knower) in getting the job done."[79] Laughter and playing games are essential parts of the creative process. Beauty, and cultivating of beauty's emergence in the world, brings pleasure.

In Proverbs 8, Wisdom, existing before the beginning of the world, testifies to being at God's side throughout the creative process.[80] And in this relationship, Wisdom follows delight or play. Like a protégé beside the maestro, "Wisdom was daily God's delight, *playing* before God always, rejoicing in God's inhabited world and delighting in the human race."[81]

Artists find passion in making art. Not only that, but art also functions as a gateway into that same creative passion. Beauty, which comes to us through the artistic fashioning of time, space, and matter wakes us up to what we love.

> The heavens are telling the glory of God;
> and the firmament proclaims his handiwork.
> Day to day pours forth speech,
> and night to night declares knowledge.
> There is no speech, nor are there words;
> their voice is not heard;
> yet their voice goes out through all the earth,
> and their words to the end of the world.
> (Psalm 19:1–4 NRSV)

Art, the stuff made by artists, is something that changes us as we see it. In other words, art puts us in play. The evidence of someone seeing with long, hard intent is the invitation to viewers to, themselves, see.

Art is not simply a product of seeing, it evokes or provokes the viewer to see. Poetry invites us to read (sense) between the lines. Songs invite us to find harmony within and beyond ourselves. Photographs and paintings help us envision an alternative to the dominant visions of our culture.

Romantics and realists have argued for over a century about whether life imitates art (meaning we only see in the natural world what artists and philosophers suggest to us) or whether art imitates life (meaning art is an attempt to copy intangible universal forms of life). But what both major arguments grant is that art has a unique and necessary relationship to life.

Art turns up the volume on life. Think again of that book, movie, painting, or concert that completely changed your life. We use language like, "took my breath away," "blew my mind," or, "I just had church," to describe the way the beauty employs our senses to change the reality or moment in which we live. Such beauty awakens us to the presence of God and God's all-encompassing dreams for creation.

My daughter is a huge fan of *Project Runway*, the cable network show that sets up twenty-some beginning designers with materials, models, and weekly elimination challenges that eventually narrow the field down to one winning designer. Watching all of the project-makeover-type shows that have since expanded from this fashion design competition to include contests between cooks, models, and artists you see that while beauty may be subjective, a field of experts typically dismiss work that does not move them. Creativity moves into beauty by putting the viewer into play as an admirer or appreciator.

Picture God making creation in those first moments, and then God admiring the beauty. Hebrew scholar Ellen Davis has put it this way:

How we see the world is how we learn to value it. And it's striking that in Genesis 1 what we know of God, really the only things we know of God, is that God creates and God values what God has made. God sees it as good, but that can also be translated, "God saw how beautiful it was." And I think there's almost an element of surprise, of delight, that . . . we know from our own smaller creations. And so God is, in a sense, the first appreciator of the world, the first one to see that it is beautiful.[82]

There is a surprise or delight when God became the "first appreciator" of the world. It is as if the work itself inspired further work. In a sense, we became God's muse. So God lovingly responded with more creating. God's own intimacy with creation inspired the expansion of creation.

This same delight of seeing things come to life is what the artist longs for. Beauty resides in the eyes of the beholder, because it is in discovering beauty that the beholder takes off her sandals. Beauty could have been there all along, but it becomes real to us as we admire it.

Jürgen Moltmann writes about the converse of this effect, "The beautiful in God is what makes us rejoice in him."[83] Beauty naturally opens up delight and play for God, and the beauty of the Creator God opens these up for us as well. God becomes our muse as well. The same Knitter who "knit us together in our mothers' wombs" (Psalm 139:13) knits us as we create, enjoying the process of picking out thread, changing knots, seeing slips, stitches, and hems become you and me. It is no wonder that many mystics describe the life of prayer as a sensually intimate relationship with God.

Learning from the Ingredients of Your Life

exercise 25

In this exercise you'll investigate the materials that you work with and how they play a role in informing your love. This will expand what you did for the exercise at the end of the last chapter into a survey of the rhythms, people, and artifacts that make up your routines.

Where do you spend your day and week?

Who are the people you share much of your time with?

In what mediums do you work?

If you aren't an artist, this last question could be tricky. Consider the *moments*, *footprints*, and *stuff* that your life entails. Whether or not you're an artist, include the mundane part of your life as well.

Now go back to the exercises from chapter 8 where you listed the things you loved (exercises 21–23). Do you see connections or points of departure between the material of your life and those things that inspire and draw you into a vision of God's loving world?

Intimacy with Our Medium

The intimacy between creator and creation does not stop at our relationship with God. As we discover the beautiful prayer we share in creating for, with, and being created by God, we learn the posture God intends for our relationship with our neighbor and all of creation.

In Fyodor Dostoevsky's *The Brothers Karamozov*, a dying priest tells the story of a boy who asks forgiveness of a dying bird. He uses the story to illustrate our responsibility to the very creation that we hold in our hands, the bed in which our foot stands. He writes, "Love all God's creation. . . . If you love everything, you will perceive the divine mystery in things. Once you perceive it, you will begin to understand it better everyday. And you will come at last to love the whole world with an all-embracing love." And echoing Jesus' words that whatever we forgive on earth is forgiven in heaven, he continues, "All things flow and are indirectly linked together, and if you push here, something will move at the other end of the world. . . . If you strike here, something somewhere will wince; if you sin here, something somewhere will suffer."[84]

On the first day of college we moved into dorms and were introduced to our roommates. For many of us it was the first time we were picked by someone or set up with someone outside of our control. It was called potluck. In a similar way, our incarnational work requires potluck matches that we do not always control. To follow God includes learning about God's dreams through the eyes of others. It's no wonder that Jesus taught his disciples to meet him in "the least of these" (Matthew 25:31–46). Collaboration as God's commissioned artists requires learning through "unearthing shared pictures of the future."[85]

In community organizing in our neighborhood we face the challenge of connecting with people who are all on different paths. Some groups organize to galvanize opposition to local pollution or political corruption. In these cases the most unlikely of partnerships across race and socioeconomics are forged to tackle the problem.

Others form into affinity groups rallying around shared paths, such as parenthood or making music. For example, a group working to bring a pizzeria or coffee shop in as commercial development typically has more expendable income, are looking for places to meet outside their home, and expect to pay a little more than average for better-than-average-quality goods and service.

But organizing around one issue or as one affinity group does not mean that people on the varied paths actually learn from one another. In their book *The Abundant Community*, Peter Block and John McKnight contrast the "common enemy" approach to community organizing with a "relationship-based" approach that values "hospitality." They write, "Community competence based on abundance is about bringing people together around possibility, not disappointment," which includes "combining our gifts and valuing association."[86] Community organizing practices such as *asset-based community development*, *appreciative inquiry*, or *place-based initiatives* all point to the importance of trusting relationships built across differences. Organizers need to get a group of diverse individuals around the table to envision and work together toward a shared outcome.

To move different groups into a shared path, we need to train ourselves to let go of prejudice and ideology until we trust one another and then feel free to move into some shared risk. Art can accomplish this by creating a shared experience that places all the viewers into a place of interpretation. If art is simply used to recruit around a cause, it is called propaganda. When art is used to appeal to a certain affinity group, it is called marketing. While propaganda and marketing employ the skills of artistic process, they do not include others outside of their goals in that process. Not only that, but when propaganda and marketing complete their tasks, the holders of the art rarely trust the process enough to take their own risks. In fact, consumers of propaganda and marketing become even further dependent upon the producers of those artifacts and less and less capable of making life for themselves. Urban organizer and poet Ross Talarico calls this "de-literacy."[87] It is the outcome of systematically taking the agency away from a citizen by co-opting or replacing all their language and symbols for external purposes.

On the other hand, community can be built through art when it disarms our prejudice, blurs our ideological barriers, and invites us into deeper relationship. Such art gifts the symbolism back to the viewer and hands the responsibility to them as co-creators.

Community-building art, then—art that resists propaganda and marketing—is about including others in the vision and in the work. When we include others in vision, it is called trust. To include others in work is to take a risk based in that trust. Imagine with me God opting out of propaganda and marketing, and instead including us as participants in visioning and in working; God opting for beauty within community by trusting and risking.

In the process, God the Artist entrusts the earth, the universe, and everything brought into being with its own stake in its future. We are drawn into creative work, reconciling work, and even our own calls to confess and change as we more deeply engage this world God is making.

As we learned in the first creation story, seed-bearing plants have to do their thing to propagate and humans, our thing. Adam and Eve are given freedom to name and roam and act with what Ellen Davis calls "skilled mastery," and to bear fruit in the same way that the blessed land in which we live multiplies.[88] Davis describes the creative footprint of the commissioned humans as "a very special place of power and privilege and responsibility in the world. But the condition for our exercise of skilled mastery is set by the prior blessing of the creatures of sea and sky, that they are to be fruitful and multiply."[89]

As bearers of God's Image, God entrusts us to be stewards of creativity. We cannot create at the expense of the wider world created to bear fruit, but instead are to create cooperatively, as an extension of that earlier commission. As the process continues, the visioning responsibility is returned to the created humans through priests, kings, and prophets until even Jesus himself extends this responsibility to all his disciples by breathing the Spirit on them. The apostles then pass the visioning responsibilities onto other Jewish women and men, until the creative work of God begins to reach past the geographical bounds of Judea to the ends of the earth and past the ideological bounds of religion to include those Gentiles, the rest of the world once seen as outside of God's work.

The challenge comes to us, God's commissioned artists. Can we create like God, in a way that invites people to pick up their own crayons and learn in the making? Can we develop collaborative practices to use along the way? The Word of God precedes us.

And so the gift of creating beauty is one of mutual appreciation. Lewis Hyde in his description of a gift economy, writes, "When we are in the spirit of the gift we love to feel the body open outward." For the gift is drawn "from plenty to emptiness" seeking "the barren, the arid, the stuck, and the poor."[90]

It is no surprise that the Son of God who would demonstrate the greatest of love, so as "to lay down one's life for one's friends," also commissioned those friends to heal the sick and raise the dead, saying, "Freely you have received; freely give" (John 15:13 NRSV, Matthew 10:8 NIV).

Framing the Design Challenge between Multiple Dreams

exercise 26

Often the hardest part of learning is surrendering deep commitments we have to unexamined assumptions or perspectives. Language such as "God's will" or the "kingdom of God" can be used as euphemisms for "my will" or the "kingdom of me." Jeremiah encouraged the exiled Hebrews to seek the welfare of others, and Jesus taught his disciples that in serving the other (the least of these), they were, in fact, serving *him*. Design thinking begins with what is called a design problem, the framing of where we want to be and where we are now. For this exercise use a comparison between your articulation of God's vision and at least two others' articulation to define a design problem.

1. **Your vantage point:** First, think of the imagery you most often use to articulate God's expanding love. What comes to mind when you think of wholeness, beauty, justice, and love? List these words on a sheet of paper and try to sketch or journal about their relationship.

2. **Another's perspective:** Interview one loved one and ask them what they dream of when you mention wholeness, beauty, justice, and God's love. List these words on a new sheet and try to sketch them from this person's perspective.

3. **An outside perspective:** Interview someone with whom you are not as close—someone who is a source of aggravation, a competitor, or perhaps an enemy—and ask them what they dream of when you mention wholeness, beauty, justice, or God's love. List these words on a new sheet and try to sketch these.

4. **Compare these three differences** (maybe you'll see others as well). A design problem is like Buckminster Fuller's example of building a bridge to get people over a river. Don't force it at this stage, but simply notice the differences between your hopes, the hopes of those you love, and the hopes of those who challenge you.

Make Your Life a Monastery

So—and yes, I'm asking—what has God to do?
What other course—His being God and All—but to renew
His lately non-too-vivid Image in the aspect of mankind,
so that, by His Icon thus restored, we dim occasions might
once more come to know Him? And how should this be done,
save by the awful advent of the very God Himself, our Lord
and King and gleaming Liberator Jesus Christ?

Here, belovéd numbskulls, is a little picture: You gather,
one presumes, what must be done when a portrait on a panel
becomes obscured—maybe even lost—to external stain.
The artist does not discard the panel, though the subject
must return to sit for it again, whereupon the likeness is
etched once more upon the same material. As He tells us in
the Gospel, I came to seek and to save that which was
lost—*our faces, say.*
    —St. Athanasios, translation by Scott Cairns[91]

If God designed vision and work to conspire within
artists so that they may continue the work of creation,
how can we intentionally join in?

This last chapter will explore the disciplines of God's
commissioned artists. It will follow the line of the lost
arts of God with which we opened the book. If you
have made this journey with me and are interested in
deepening your acquaintance with this creative God
or more deeply integrating this story of faith with your

everyday practices, then this final chapter is where the rubber hits the road.

Throughout this book I have worked around the modern mechanics of God's work to "seek and to save the lost." As I stated at the beginning, I believe this book's contents can coexist with many paradigms. My experience as a follower of Jesus partnering with groups ranging widely both theologically and culturally, is that few of us dare to risk being drawn into new concepts if they do not reinforce our existing ones. In this case, story and metaphor are more effective tools for building an appreciative community of creative risk takers (or building a community of readers, in our case). In short, our dogma can be one of the greatest obstacles to getting on the magic carpet of loving creative participation with God. However, I begin this final chapter with a poem translated from the ancient work of St. Athanasios to finally address that question of God's agency in our salvation.

In the panel described above by Athanasios, vision meets work and creation expands. The ancient theologian frames the incarnation as God entering into the art to sit for us artists who may find our truest callings by emulating and bearing the image of God. Consider this idea next to Elaine Scarry's proposal that art involves observing beauty with the willingness to change one's position, and there we have the heart of the matter.

Jesus Christ is the expression of God's desire for our fullest life as creators. As such, worship, the art of the church, shapes Jesus' apprentices through the integration of God's dreams and the work of imagination and the everyday craft. Throughout our lives, God activates our potential by placing creative choices ahead of us to "create a future distinct from the past."[92] We realize that future by acting on those choices.

Our beauty is our creator's intention, and so the transformation of those beautiful things gone awry is also the desire of the Creator. God's vision is for everything and everyone, the 99 percent and the 1 percent. "God is not willing that any should perish." Our visages as image bearers of God are made new as we intentionally engage this re-creating God.

Like Harold with his crayon, each step of our life unfolds as we take steps to engage life with intention. Like a guitar string, we resonate as we are set off by the harmonics around us. Faith is a gift as free as a song. And the great Conductor/ Composer's deepest desire is that all creation reverberate with that song.

God makes an even grander bet than Harold, diving into the unfolding divine vision, schooling us in that posture of trusting beauty's "drawing-in capacity." But it all takes discipline. It doesn't happen by accident or (at least not in my experience) by sudden, divine miracle. I suppose that there have been poets who woke up one morning, put pen to paper for the first time, and wrote gorgeous sonnets. But art does not usually work that way.

We need disciplines.

For millennia, monks have known that growth most often occurs where seeds have been planted and well cared for. Consider a few biblical examples. Abraham put vision to work, packing up his wife and the band of servants and cattle, setting out from the familiar Ur into an unknown land that God promised to "show" him. From there, the grand story of progeny, land, and Israel's twelve tribes unfolded. Alone in Ur, with no action, the story would remain flat. Moses, too, put vision to work. He turned aside to see the burning bush and the story magically unfolded. But it was as he entered Egypt, confronting Pharaoh, organizing the weary slaves, that the epic story of God's deliverance of Israel unfolded. As a form of performance art, Ezekiel lay in the public square on his left side for 390 days straight, and then on his right side for 40 more days. As the curious tried to make sense of Ezekiel's art, they were rewarded with further insight into God's dreams. Peter dropped his nets and allowed his story to unfold. His response to follow differentiates the good news of Jesus Christ from the news of others who either had few followers or had no dissent in their group. Jesus' own decision at Gethsemane—"Not my will but thine"—demonstrated that discipline, response, and action are necessary in this human/material plane for God's will to become reality.

Scripture also shares stories of when God's bet on beauty has failed. Jesus told many parables, and those without ears would misconstrue or just disregard them. Jesus couldn't perform miracles in his own hometown. And some audiences of the disciple's own healing campaign would not respond, leading Jesus to instruct his apprentices to shake the dust off their feet and go where they could catch traction, where their audiences could get drawn in.

At times we draw God in through our own engagement. Abraham made a case to God for Sodom and God jumped into the bargaining. The Hebrew women in Egypt cried out under oppression and God responded with the Exodus. The people in Judges cried out under oppression and God showed up. The Syrophoenician woman bargained and bantered with Jesus until he agreed to cast a demon out of her daughter (Mark 7:25–30).

For some of us these stories presents a conflict between our prayer—"Your will be done on earth as it is in heaven"—and God's sovereign capacity to answer that prayer.[93] Yet, in all these cases, the attraction between the messenger and audience determine how long lived the message will be.

It's like the negative and positive sides of a magnet, except magnetism seems too mechanical a language for it. Art gives us fields for thinking about this more organically. Think of the watercolorist who adds paint to the edge of an already wet line. She dips the hairs of the brush into the thick plum red and sets it on the sienna line. Like slow suction, the burnt orange emerges. The color is drawn in. Did the water draw that line or did the artist? The fine craft of watercolor required the artisan to conspire with the materials. What materials seem to creatively conspire with your work? What materials around you are creatively conspiring with the dreams of God?

Does creativity actually bring us deeper into communion with God and more aligned with our calling within God's grand work of art? And if so, what practices influence or strengthen this creative way of life?

Almost monthly I walk into an enormous gothic-shaped white-walled cathedral flooded by fresh sunlight that pours through cobalt blue and fuchsia modern-edged stained glass. Sitting under the wooden rafters, I hear the braided voices of about forty men bouncing between the walls, chanting something like:

> O God come to my assistance
> O Lord, make haste to help me
> Glory be to the Father, and to the Son,
>   and to the Holy Spirit.
> The God who was, and is, and is to come
> at the end of the ages.

I always look forward to this regular pilgrimage to the Monastery of the Holy Spirit, about an hour's drive from my downtown home in Atlanta. It is an embodied lesson in contrast for me. My life in the city and theirs in the cloister—the noises, colors, lines, and pace—stand in stark contrast. The monks there are part of a fifteen-hundred-year-old rite of singing the psalms eight times a day. Many have called this practice "inhabiting" the psalms.

Their space even bears the marks of minimalist intention, paying careful attention to lines, curves, contrast, and color— or lack of color. Whitewashed fences and white concrete and marble allow the eye to rest and observe the careful cuts or unique additions or flair. The men in the monastery wear the same white-and-black garb laid out by their founder, St. Benedict, in 529 AD. They work as a co-op, dividing labor and organizing tasks together. And yet their day is segmented, much like many Muslims and Jews, with regular hours of prayer. Every three hours they drop their work and sing the psalms, and then return to work, or sleep, depending on time of day. Even their music is shaped by this minimalist intention; they sing Gregorian chants that return to the same note for 85 percent of a given melody.

The Benedictine monastic tradition is based on a rule of life. In the late fifth century, Benedict and his colleagues saw an influx of children to their monasteries. These youth were abandoned or sent away because of the harsh conditions of urban life. The monks had a hard time instructing these youth in the ascetic life or even in shared communal responsibility. Benedict's response was to design a set of practices that would govern their life and shape them into people of prayer and humility. Benedict realized that routines and environments shape our imaginations, and these monks at the monastery I visit carry out his design to this day.

My visits have gotten me thinking about the correlation between a monastery and an art studio. Many artists are first trained in the classics, until their own understanding of the material and the technique is taken for granted. Both abbots and artists intentionally design space and rhythms that lead to a particular life. Like a member of a religious order, the watercolorist intentionally places her brush into the desired color, places her desk in a desired way, and creates a studio that draws out the desired results. She pays attention to her materials, her space, her posture. The musician practices scales. The actor carefully researches and studies the lives of his characters. The studio and the monastery, though seemingly opposite because one seems adaptive and the other unchanging, both demonstrate the outcome of intentional life.

So what is your life's studio like? What do you pay attention to? How would you be your own Benedict, making a rule for your life?

What would it look like to make your life a monastery, intentionally applying vision to your work of time, space, and matter? And more than simply being intentional about the power your choices have on physical environments, consider what intention you breathe into your interpersonal relationships.

To clarify this point, bring to mind how time, space, and matter are the ingredients of God's art. They inform our art as well. In the words of Wendell Berry, our consistent commitment to a certain context, to consistent seasons, and to a certain medium can inform our "art of being here."

This process requires thoughtful care. David Byrne, the front man of the Talking Heads, suggests that our attention to environments determines what can emerge, that creation actually "happens in reverse." For example, the grand hall of La Scala was particularly designed by Wagner to bring lower-end instruments into the opera house, while the intimate halls in which Mozart performed enabled him to design compositions with more key changes and subtleties. Smaller clubs can accentuate jazz while larger spaces lend themselves to arena rock. If you try to put music in a place ill fit for it, the sounds can bleed and slur or simple tempos and chord structures will feel mundane. Byrne even cites the naturalistic example of the Scarlet Tanagers in San Francisco that have changed the pitch of their songs over the course of forty years to be heard above the increased noise of pedestrians. He writes:

> It seems that creativity is adaptive, like anything else. When a space becomes available, work emerges to fill it. The genius, the emergence of a truly remarkable and memorable work, happens when the thing is perfectly suited to its context and is also surprising. And when something works, it strikes us as not just being clever—a good adaptation—but as strongly and emotionally resonant. When the right thing is in the right place we are moved.[94]

So, how have you noticed your song changing throughout your life? And does your song resonate with your current environment?

Byrne notes that your environment has a surprisingly deep influence on that change. Poet George MacDonald describes the environment as home: "In the perfect time, O perfect God / When we are in our home . . . / When joy shall carry every sacred load . . . / What if thou make us able to make like thee?"[95] Somehow, when we are truly home, carried by God's joyous love, we awaken to the call to create. Take a look at your environment through Benedict's eyes and ask yourself, what does my environment make my song into? Do you see the influence you can have over your life's shape by attending to your practices and your intentional environments? Whether you view yourself in control of these factors or passively receiving life (for we are always somehow vacillating between both) notice the story your environment is telling. Does it evoke more creation?

Eastern forms of Christianity often describe worship as the animating or enlivening of creation. What do you do with the creation that is at your disposal? How you answer these questions will lead you to what your rule of life should be. Consider how time, space, and matter are gifts to be invested in this creative enterprise as God's commissioned artist. Trust what resonates. Scrap what seems ill fitting for your time or context. Listen for how the whole is part of God's All-in-All. Make a studio of your life!

(Wave 1 of 6)

Dreaming: prayer requests, meditations, and brainstorms

As with the monks, through much of Christian history, prayer has been viewed as formational. Even though modern culture frequently stereotypes monks as being escapist, there is something more going on under the surface. Many monks and nuns organize their lives like an extended yoga class, as a series of postures that embed themselves and others in the story that they seek. Their rituals are that "available space" that David Byrne spoke of.

This concept of a prayer practice is a recently new idea to me. My earliest memories of prayer were petition. My parents and extended family set extraordinary examples of devotion and commitment to God. I remember beginning and ending every meal as a child around my family's dining room table, beseeching God to bless our efforts, our family, and the "hands of those who prepared" our meals. Whether or not it was my parents' intentions, this practice always felt to me like a posture of making ourselves small, like a young athlete trying to avoid eye contact with a coach in fear of being called on to do something.

I also remember growing up with prayer request time in Sunday school. This was typically a time for people to list the things that broke their hearts, that made them uneasy, or that represented whatever evil and injustice they hoped to end. We wanted someone (God, specifically) to do something about what we saw and dreamt after. This prayer *was* a practice as well. But instead of being a prayer that drew me into responsibility or partnership, these prayers felt to me like a child asking for more allowance, or a team throwing a Hail Mary pass when they're down by two touchdowns with too little time left to play.

Note the role of imagination in these prayer postures. Petition, as I practiced as a child, was a posture that took the ability to act on our imaginations away from the artist. Asking permission to do our work takes away the very capacity of taking a leap. Granted, surrender involved in petition as one of many postures of prayer makes great sense, but knowing when to surrender responsibility is key. When petition is the only posture, it changes our song into something passive and disengaged; it creates a victim complex. This is similar to what Peter Block calls limiting stories, "personal versions of the past" that reinforce inaction or "those that are rehearsed to make the point that the future will be a slightly modified continuation of the past out of which the story arose."[96] As most any therapist will tell you, your habits and inner critics are often the largest obstacles to real change. It's worth being intentional about how prayer is used to limit or to expand.

Petition, however, need not be the norm and certainly not the only shape of prayer. Prayer for the monk is not a transactional situation but rather a transformational one. Like an artist entering a studio, the praying follower of Jesus is creating a space, with a plausibility structure, within which God's reality is known more fully through the material space of his or her life.

Jesus, knowing the formational role of prayer, taught his apprentices a dream, a story, a vision to repeat. That prayer also began with a vision—the God with whom we are invited to relate in an intimate, familial way, is honored. In a sense, we begin by honoring God as parent. And then we invite that God to visit his heavenly reign on earth physically, socially, psychologically, and holistically. When we pray, "Your kingdom come, your will be done on earth as it is in heaven," we are training our minds to anticipate God's creative work, fashioning the present time, space, and matter into something resonant with the abundant self-transcending love of God. In many ways the Lord's Prayer is a vision, a dream of what we'll be doing when it is accomplished, and a plea that God be drawn back into the work.

Granted, the Lord's Prayer includes transactional aspects such as "give us" and "forgive us." And yet, both generosity and forgiveness are placed within a narrative as well. The qualifier, "Give us today our daily bread," is infused with vision—a world, like manna in the wilderness, where nourishment comes in single servings for everyone, never running out, but never hoarded. The forgiveness that is asked for is drawn forth from a sort of intraforgiving cosmos—God forgiving others, even while we are forgiving others. Jesus' prayer is designed as a practice meant to reduce the separation of forgiveness's consumers and producers.

Block writes that "the essence of creating an alternative future [distinct from the past] comes from citizen-to-citizen engagement that constantly focuses on the wellbeing of the whole."[97] As suggested by the Lord's Prayer, the dreaming involved in the creative process is strongest when focus is on the well-being of all of God's creation. It's later, in the hovering stage, that we focus in for our own particular project.

The early Christians admonished one another to "set their minds" on certain things, to "take every thought captive," and to savor—to "taste and see"—the goodness of the Lord. If you are an artisan, listen to the chords of your guitar, to the echoes of the rooms in which you play, look at the colors spilling onto your drafting table, get to know the characters that are unfolding as you write, watch the way that the wind hits the fabric you weave. These experiences are access points to the dreams of God, what Jesus proclaimed as the "kingdom of God," God's reach, and—by extension—your reach. You can shape your imagination in this reach by meditating on those things "of heaven" and integrating them with your lived reality.

Dallas Willard has said this about such a vision in our lived material reality:

To live strongly and creatively in the kingdom of the heavens, we need to have firmly fixed in our minds what our future is to be like. We want to live fully in the kingdom now. . . . In this way our future can be incorporated into our life now and our life now can be incorporated into our future. . . . [This] material universe is both an essential display of the greatness and goodness of God and the arena of the eternal life of finite spirits, including the human."[98]

The place of dreaming is one where we experience God and can serve as access points for other people to experience God.

The prophets would tell of a time when God's commissioning spirit would hover over all people, when "sons and daughters will prophesy . . . old men will dream dreams . . . young men will see visions" (Joel 2:28 NIV). They gave God's commissioned artists a vision for an eternally unfolding future when God "creates the heavens and earth all over again," where we will "rejoice forever" in what God creates, a time when the vision of truth and mercy integrate in God. When all creatures "will transmit the vision of God throughout all of the earth, and all humanity will come regularly to the center of divine presence on earth, to delight in God and worship him (from Isaiah 65–66)."[99]

What do you dream about? Can you see all that resonates with the story of God entering creation to suffer and create with us and to bring all things to their fullness? What harmony, hue, or texture harmonizes with God's grand imagination? What is piquing yours?

If you are a parent or teacher, look at your kids, watch them play, fight, sleep, stumble clumsily. What in them already rings true? What do they dream of?

If you are a resident of a neighborhood or a regular at a pub, pay attention to the witty banter, to the concerns and joys of the people around you. How is God creating these people? How are they creating you?

After looking at the way things are on this earth, here's what I've decided is the best way to live: Take care of yourself, have a good time, and make the most of whatever job you have for as long as God gives you life. And that's about it. That's the human lot. Yes, we should make the most of what God gives, both the bounty and the capacity to enjoy it, accepting what's given and delighting in the work. It's God's gift! God deals out joy in the present, the now. It's useless to brood over how long we might live. (Ecclesiastes 5:18–20 MSG)

Dreaming involves both a suspension of reality and a mapping of what is possible. Enjoy the day the God has made . . . imagine what is yet to come!

A Collage of Your Vision

exercise 27

In this exercise you'll compare and contrast the images of God's dreams and your own projects. To prepare for this exercise, go into your journal and reread your dream journals (exercises 2 and 3) from chapter 1 and your visioning exercises (21–23) from chapter 8. Then grab a magazine and cut out pictures that depict the monastery that you are making.

St. Benedict and others who have organized monastic orders often call their rhythms a rule of life. Pastor Marjorie J. Thompson suggests three questions to consider in forming a rule of life:

1. What am I deeply attracted to and why?
2. Where do I feel God is calling me to stretch and grow?
3. What kind of balance do I need in my life?[100]

Take the pictures you cut out and design a collage that answers these three questions. You'll use this collage for the remaining exercises of this final chapter.

Hovering: put a halo on it

In his paraphrase of Paul's list of the fruit of the Spirit to the Galatians, Eugene Peterson translates *goodness* as "a conviction that a basic holiness permeates things and people" (Galatians 5:22 MSG). This conviction is a key to creating in the way that the Spirit of God creates. To hover is to assume that all materials at hand are a gift to be enjoyed.

The Spirit hovered over both the unlikely shepherd boy David and the Galilean baptized in the muddy Jordan River. Like a mother is strengthened when she appreciates the gift of everyone around the table, and a community is strengthened when they appreciate the asset of each person in their community, the spiritually creative life orbits around everything in reach, seeing its potential. I imagine that orbit being a sort of halo, a conviction that this is hallowed ground.

Creatives often call this stage of the process *incubation*, a time when the "empty place between sensing a problem and intuiting a solution . . . goes underground for a while."[101] It is counterintuitive because the creative has to trust in abundance even when she may have nothing. One academic creative accomplishes this sort of "mental meandering" by walking:

> One of the values to walking to work is mental meandering. . . . This creativity had to be a profoundly wasteful process. And that mental meandering, mind wandering and so on, is an essential process. If you are allowing that mentation to be driven by the radio or television or other people's conversations, you are just cutting down on your . . . intellectual exploratory time.[102]

Hovering is about being contented with what you find along the way, instead of forcing answers to our curiosities. The prayer, "Give us today our daily bread," is a way of hovering or suspending the inner critic who asks, "Will there be enough in the future?" Solomon, credited with authoring Ecclesiastes, wrote that, "God deals out joy in the present." Artists are courageously present because they are unafraid of mistakes or really rough drafts. Similarly, creative faith dismisses that inner critic and trusts God to draw us in. Hovering is an antidote to the kind of faith that micromanages God's commission or cuts off the freedom of the apprentice.

Daniel Lanois and Brian Eno are renowned producers of albums including U2's *The Joshua Tree* and Emmylou Harris's *Wrecking Ball*. In Lanois's documentary on beauty, *Here Is What Is,* Eno says that the magic of art is that it comes from nothing. He says:

> Beautiful things come out of shit. . . . Nobody ever believes that. . . . If you walk around with the idea that there are some people who are so gifted—they have these wonderful things in their head, but you're not one of them, you're just sort of a normal person, you could never do anything like that—then you live a different kind of life. You could have another kind of life, where you can say, "Well, I know that things come from nothing very much, and start from unpromising beginnings, and I'm an unpromising beginning, and I could start something."
>
> You know, the tiniest seed in the right situation turns into the most beautiful forest, and then the most promising seed in the wrong situation turns into nothing. And I think this would be important for people to understand, because it gives people confidence in their own lives to know that that's how things work.[103]

What practices help you suspend judgment? What practices help you bless the other without pigeonholing or objectifying them? How do you remain open to transformation? And how do your practices contribute to a confidence that you could be creative, without the extra anxiety, ambition, or acquisitiveness that often blocks up creativity? How does your practice hallow the space that allows you to be drawn further into God's expanding beautiful creation?

Awe as a Form of Hovering

A friend of mine has been a regular reminder to me this year of the practice of awe. He's been meditating through scripture on all of the times that biblical characters are "amazed" and filled with wonder.

Miriam, the sister of Moses, sang a song of amazement at the works of God delivering them from their oppressor (Exodus 15:11). The people of Israel stood in awe of the leadership gifts of Joshua and Moses (Joshua 4:14). God taught the prophet Habbakuk to learn through "amazement" at the work God was about to do with the nations around him (Habakkuk 1:5). When John the Baptist's father was cured from being mute, everyone was in awe (Luke 1:65). When Jesus healed the paralytic dropped through the roof, everyone was in awe (Matthew 9:8). The people in Jerusalem were in awe of the impact that the early church was having (Acts 2:43).

What gives you pause and wonder? What are you amazed by?

Does your day have space for this sort of wonder? Does your career, church, neighborhood, or family support this freedom to be surprised, or do these lull you into places of accommodation? Hovering is an expectation that God can do more than we ask or imagine. And so to hover is to be surprised. Jewish scholar and civil rights activist Abraham Joshua Heschel once described his sense of wonder as a "maladjusted" posture to society:

(Wave 2 of 6)

An individual dies when he ceases to be surprised. What keeps me alive—spiritually, emotionally, intellectually—is my ability to be surprised. I say, I take nothing for granted. I am surprised every morning that I see the sun shine again. When I see an act of evil, I am not accommodated—I don't accommodate myself to the violence that goes on everywhere. I'm still surprised. That's why I'm against it; why I can fight against it. We must learn how to be surprised, not to adjust ourselves.[104]

Awe is a place of differentiation where we are in the world and yet not of the world. "In order to imagine the unimaginable," psychologist Edwin Friedman writes, "people must be able to separate themselves from surrounding processes before they can even begin to see (or hear) things differently."[105]

And *awe* is not the only hovering posture: Mary *pondered*, Jesus *withdrew* to a lonely place, the shepherds at Jesus' birth announcement and the disciples in the upper room were *terrified*. The disciples were invited to *bless* on earth those things to be blessed in heaven. Our job is to put a halo on more and more, expecting it to be an easel for God's next act!

Patience as a Form of Hovering

> If the world were merely seductive, that would be easy. If it were merely challenging, that would be no problem. But I arise in the morning torn between a desire to improve the world and a desire to enjoy the world. This makes it hard to plan the day.
> —E. B. White[106]

Hovering is also, finally, about *patience*. Sometimes the things we are meant to make require time—lots and lots of time. Rushing into a quick judgment can actually cut the creative process short.

When Johnny Cash was writing the title track for his apocalyptic and morose album, *American IV: The Man Comes Around,* he couldn't shake the song from his head for three months. He created over three dozen pages of lyrics before weeding them down to the final song. Leonard Cohen wrote more than eighty verses to his song "Hallelujah" before settling on those on his 1984 album *Various Positions.* This book sat in notes and meanderings for eight years before I found a publisher ready to run with it, and it then took another year or two of writing, editing, and rewriting before it was published.

Hovering can be a place of prayer. In the Hebrew wisdom tradition are many forms of prayer. Both ecstatic praise and existential lamentation emerge in the uninhibited space of Hebrew prayer. And so in one song the psalmist can pray both, "Shout Hallelujah, you God-worshipers. . . . He has never let you down, never looked the other way," and, "God, God . . . my God! Why did you dump me miles from nowhere? Doubled up with pain, I call to God all the day long. No answer. Nothing" (Psalm 22 MSG).

The psalmists access the place below the surface without regard to the critical eyes of the theologian or civil authorities. As these are bound in the community hymnal, the children of Israel bind their patient affirmation of God's promises to their active demanding engagement with God. Their patience is infused with active imagination, an audacious claim on God for the realization of that dream.

Put Halos on Your Vision

exercise 28

There have been two texts that we have returned to throughout this book as examples of the dreams of God: the metaphor of the fruit growing from a Holy Spirit–inspired tree and the prophetic story of a new way of life depicted by

Isaiah and read by Jesus as he began his ministry (see Psalm 1 and Galatians 5, or Isaiah 61). Pick one of these and then look over the collage in exercise 27. Take some time to think playfully over your collage, seeing unknown connections. Draw halos or doves over those things in your life that fit the passage you have chosen. If you're studying this book with friends, offer observations to each other about their rule-of-life collages and the text you've chosen.

Risking: daring to find God's voice in yours

I struggle with nerve. In an almost Jekyll-and-Hyde fashion, I am at one moment enthusiastically leading the charge, only to be deflated and lost moments later. My intuition can lead me to great moments of courage and leadership, and then I find myself like Harold with the purple crayon, wandering and looking for the way back to the familiar.

I think a lot of creatives are familiar with this struggle. Paul Simon sings that trusting intuition is "just like going fishing / you cast a line and hope you get a bite."[107] On stage or in the studio we come alive, and then, when the muse leaves and the silence ensues, we drift into places of fear and awkward self-consciousness. So risk, for the creative, can be a precarious part of life.

As a young teenager I learned the risk of trusting intuition through performing music, mountain climbing, and selling shoes at a running store. Just like repeatedly playing a song teaches the guitarist confidence, so did taking larger and larger leaps and risking helping strangers find products to improve their own skills help me find confidence. Sometimes I'd lose a sale. Sometimes I'd embarrass myself in a concert. And a few times I got physically injured. I discovered the painful costs of overestimating my strengths, and yet I grew through each test of my limits. And life and art continue to be a lesson in risk.

A few years ago I was to play in a festival in Cincinnati, Ohio, and was couch surfing at a friend's house. He was renting the house from a music producer who lived next door and happened to be completing the production on an album with David Wilcox that same week. Wilcox is a proven singer-songwriter whom I've followed with appreciation since college. I got to meet David briefly early in the day and we had a short conversation during which he tried out some jokes that would likely end up in his show the following night. Later that afternoon, after returning to the house to hang with my friends, I had the place to myself and began to practice for my show. While I practiced, David came across the lawn to the house and knocked on the door, asking if he could listen in. There I was, faced with the opportunity to play for one of my early heroes, right there in my friend's living room.

In that chance to play, paired with Wilcox's gracious, encouraging smile, I had to draw on all I knew about risk. I had to play with my whole heart, to enter into the creative space without regard to what he may think or say. As it turned out, we spent the next two hours passing the guitar back and forth and playing songs reflecting on approaches and tone and hooks. He was generous and truly entered into the space *with* me, as genuinely present as he is in any show.

During that time he shared something that has hung with me ever since. He said he came over that evening because my *voice* called him in. There had been nothing noteworthy in our conversation earlier that day, but as he heard my voice singing he said it rang with confidence and pull and it drew him into a place of curiosity. And as I thought of it, I discovered I could say the same thing about other creative projects. Resonance has always been what wakes me up as a speaker or singer or

pastor. The emotional courage necessary to risk leaping into
that place of song is connected to a curious uncertainty and my
own awareness of a deeper song. In his book *A Failure of Nerve*,
Edwin Friedman writes this about the emotional requirements
to taking risk:

> The acceptance and even cherishing of uncertainty
> is critical to keeping the human mind from voyaging
> into the delusion of omniscience. The willingness to
> encounter serendipity is the best antidote we have for
> arrogance of thinking we know. . . . Related here is the
> necessity of preserving ambiguity in artistic expression
> since, if the viewer's imagination is to flower, it is
> important not to solve the problem in advance.[108]

Since that surprise encounter with a mentor songwriter, I
continue to follow my voice's call and learn my limits through
an openness to serendipity. I fail often! But the confidence to
risk is rooted in an experience of a deep swelling song—the
song that pulls us into a deeper and deeper resonance if we but
let go of our "delusions of omniscience."

One more personal anecdote to make an even finer point
about risk comes from a retreat I took in west Texas. It was
a long-awaited rest after a year of late-night prayers longing
for direction from God. I had *hovered* for way too long, it
felt. I came to a lush space where the rivers run through the
crevasses of the foothills to meet other artists and pastors. I
rested, canoed, wrote music, smoked cigars, and laughed with
a company of like-minded strangers.

While there I struck up a friendship with a woman, a painter
who was my senior by a good thirty years. She and I would talk
about artistic process: hers, the attention to colors, mine, the
attention to resonance. One day over lunch, after having built
some rapport, she spoke to me directly about the longing she
saw in my eyes, and asked fairly poignantly about the prayers

I had been praying for those months before, the laments I thought God had never heard.

She offered words of encouragement and she kept reflecting on the deep love of God. It was refreshing. Then she shared a challenge. In the conversation she painted a word-image of a boy in my inner-city neighborhood approaching me to ask why I do what I do as pastor, neighbor, and community agency director. In this future she was painting, that boy would ask, "Do you do this because of Jesus?" Her words spoke indirectly to my confidence to take risks. While I am a person of faith, I've accumulated a great deal of scar tissue in my heart over various coercive forms of evangelism, so her story was touching on a nerve. She went further and suggested that I'd probably be tempted to blow it off in a nonchalant way, deferring to him by asking him what he thought. "But," she warned, "you *know* you do." Her deep, perceiving azure eyes peered into me and called out that same voice of which Wilcox had spoken. She knew that God's deep love was a source of confidence for what I wanted to do and who I wanted to become, that "inner voice given at birth" that Parker Palmer described.

Since then I've begun to indentify hesitation in my life as coming from a couple of primary causes: either I'm hesitant to take a risk because I don't want my vision to be criticized or I'm not sure if the work I'm attempting will accomplish my grandiose vision. In each case my lack of confidence comes from confusing my identity (as God's artwork) with my vision (as God's apprentice discovering God's voice through my artwork). Like the difference between dampening a piano string and pushing the sustain pedal to let it ring, my hands were clinging too tightly to the string of my life, preventing it from resonating with God's all-consuming chord. My pride or insecurity keep me from participating in the unfolding dreams of God.

Jesus taught about confidence in the face of risk. Using the imagery of the plowing device designed to leverage the combined strength of farm animals, he invited his followers into an integrative life of participation in *his* yoke, not plowing endlessly alone. In that proverbial sense of many hands making light work, he described working with him as easy and light. He was always taking risks with his yoke, though.

Just days before his betrayal he sent some of his servants to ask for a colt to ride into town and others to get a room for the Passover. Apprentices who would jump into his large art project had to leave their father and mother, had to let go of their nets, and had to leave behind good job security. And by the time of Pentecost, the early church was following in his risky steps, unplugging from all sorts of other safety nets. They saw the kingdom of God as reality, something at hand, in their moment. The real risk, they saw, was to follow their voice, the calling of God in their lives. As we noted earlier, "Discovering vocation does not mean scrambling toward some prize just beyond my reach but accepting the treasure of true self I already possess."[109] For Jesus and his followers, this risk would come at great cost, but its possibility was rooted in the deep, resonant dreams of God for all time.

Being drawn into risk has to do with this deep rootedness. The visions or dreams that we act on are not motivated by shame or fame. They well up from below, from a deep-seated knowing.

Designing Your 40-Day Pilot Project   exercise 29

It's time to start a forty-day pilot project or a prototype. This will require your collage and the list of your life's ingredients from exercise 25. Rules of life can be as rigorous or as simple as you need. Martin Luther King Jr. had ten rules for all those who joined his movement, including things such as, "Meditate daily on the teachings and life of Jesus," "Walk and talk in a manner of love, for God is love," and "Refrain from violence of fist, tongue, or heart."[110] When Lou Reed was part of Andy Warhol's Velvet Underground it is said that Warhol required five new songs a day from him. Rules of Life usually benefit from transparency with at least one other person (probably not your life partner or supervisor). Think whom that person(s) would be and invite them to meet up so you can share your project before you begin, and after the forty days are over. Their perspective can usually help you in the estimation of your project goals and in evaluating the outcomes. Timelines are also helpful, so limit the project to these forty days.

For this project, choose a practice that you would engage daily. You may have a creative project that you have postponed or procrastinated on. You may want to partner with a few other people in a collaborative project—if so, be cognizant of your daily commitment and your limits when you design the project. If a project does not come to mind, you may want to repeat one of the exercises that you've already tried in this book. You can find a list of the exercises in the Index on page 199.

Flannery O'Connor wrote, "Art never responds to the wish to make it democratic; it is not for everybody; it is only for those who are willing to undergo the effort needed to understand it."[111] The growth of the creative life in the Way of Jesus is similarly connected to the effort to understand the connection between our dreams and our work, God's dreams and God's work.

Listening: the voice of God in and through creation

Risks that are good well up from a vision or dream of God's intentions. Not all risk is virtuous. Pride and hubris are examples of risk that harms, that misshapes God's creation. And so the dreamer who hovers and then risks must stay in constant conversation with God and with life.

To explain this conversation we need to return for a moment to the type of dreaming that God demonstrates. God did not dream of a world that was somehow separate, or at a distance. The Triune God, in a dance of mutual submission, dreamt of a world with whom God would relate. In fact, at each point that you or I separate ourselves from this shared world, we experience a sort of emptiness, a void, an unreconciled place.

With this note, it is understandable why Dietrich Bonhoeffer, a German theologian who founded an intentional community, wrote his strong refute of idealistic visionaries who point to their riskiness as proof of their authority. Such people create silos between their vision and the rest of community:

> In Christian brotherhood everything depends upon being clear right from the beginning . . . that Christian brotherhood is not an ideal, but a divine reality. . . . God hates visionary dreaming; it makes the dreamer proud and pretentious. The man who fashions a visionary ideal of community demands that it be realized by God, by others, and by himself. . . . When his ideal picture is destroyed, he sees the community going to smash. So he becomes, first an accuser of his brethren, then an accuser of God, and finally the despairing accuser of himself.[112]

Bonhoeffer, through his experience of the Third Reich, saw how vision can be a form of idolatry, oppression, and even fascism. Pride and pretention separate such a visionary from the community, God, and the self. So even the mastery of the ego or the flesh becomes a form of violence against God's creative purpose. Such a person cannot hear his limits from others, even from his own intuition, and workaholism, judgmentalism, and idolatry ensue.

The art of *listening* is the process of understanding the stuff or matter you're engaging. Do you remember Mother Teresa and how she prayed in a way that both she and God were listening? Listening is a lot like being in a prayer group with everyone and everything around you, but it is not the kind of prayer group where everyone is talking over each other and leaves feeling unheard. Rather, listening is a process, an ebb and flow, a giving and receiving, a learning relationship. That is what I always imagine the monks are doing at the monastery in those early morning hours chanting psalms. Artists have a similar relationship to their work.

Andy Goldsworthy is a naturalist sculptor and installation artist who brings the commonplace leaf or stone into conversation with surrounding landscapes. On one occasion retold through the documentary *Rivers and Tides* Goldsworthy sits on a gray Nova Scotia beach constructing a five-foot-tall cone-shaped sculpture by stacking rings made from small slabs of slate found strewn across the shore. The documentary shows the sculpture failing day after day, before its eventual completion. As viewers, we get an insight into Goldsworthy's process—both the work and the vision involved in selecting pieces and ordering their placement, as well as the grief that comes when the integrity of a sculpture fails.

He reflects on the learning process of his relationship with his material:

The moment something collapses it is intensely disappointing. This is the fourth time [the sculpture has] fallen and each time I got to know the stone a little bit more. It got higher each time, so it grew in proportion to my understanding of the stone. That is really one of the things my art is trying to do. It is trying to understand the stone. I obviously don't understand it well enough yet.[113]

Goldsworthy remained courageous, even as his imperfection was on display. He left his definition of the outcome open to discovery. The creative in the art of God must not think so highly of himself that his courage depends upon self-sufficiency and isolation. Our creativity is not rooted in our untetheredness.

Our untetheredness frees us to be creative and learn in the process. The creative life in God necessarily incorporates the creative work of others. Henri Nouwen has written about it this way:

If we do not know we are the beloved sons and daughters of God, we're going to expect someone in the community to make us feel that way. They cannot. We'll expect someone to give us that perfect, unconditional love. But community is not loneliness grabbing onto loneliness: "I'm so lonely, and you're so lonely." It's solitude grabbing onto solitude: "I am the beloved; you are the beloved; together we can build a home." Sometimes you are close, and that's wonderful. Sometimes you don't feel much love, and that's hard. But we can be faithful. We can build a home together and create space for God and for the children of God. Within the discipline of community are the disciplines of forgiveness and celebration.[114]

Forgiveness and celebration are forms of listening. Without them our visions skew toward our isolated individualistic ideals. In a world of our own ideals we judge everyone who falls short, and eventually we fall under our own judgment and shame. At times we even co-opt God as the licenser of such judgment. This kills our song, it steals our laughter, it banishes the muse.

Our freedom to fail and to learn without pride getting in the way is found in the grace of our given calling, to be in the process of learning. Like Goldsworthy sees his art, as a public exploration of trying to understand stone, so God has commissioned us as artisans to understand our neighbor and ourselves, and to understand the God who continues to create us.

We had a practice at Neighbors Abbey called a listening group. For an hour a week we practiced a prayer process of letting go. In the first twenty minutes we sat in silence like the Spirit of God who sat over the waters, listening without trying to size things up. Then we'd invite one member of the group to share and observe his or her life, anything that came to mind. For the remainder of our hour the group's job would be to sit with that story and make observations, dismissing the temptation to editorialize or resolve what that person had shared.

One week a participant, let's call her Gayle, had a series of challenges that she could not fix: her roles as a partner, a mentor, and a former business colleague all seemed in turmoil. As she shared these things it felt similar to watching Goldsworthy's sculptures collapse: each one brought a grief, each one felt like the end of the rope. Finally she explained, "The big issue is that I'm powerless to fix any of these!" When she said this she sighed. And as she did we all felt the room change with her. You could sense the powerlessness open to a space of surrender. And, like a rappeller taking the first lean back into the harness, she was held by something other than her work or her vision. This is that moment between risking and reintegrating, the space between starting to make and completing a particular work of art.

Listening for Those Things That Must Return to Ashes

In design, the risk stage is usually followed by some sort of *evaluation*. Short, low-risk experiments (often called rapid prototypes) followed by a quick evaluation can train individuals and groups to stay in the creative zone without every idea being shut down because of perceived high risks. One church I know of in an affluent southern city has over five hundred lawyers participating in their congregation. Imagine the risk aversion of such a community! Their pastor told me that any action they take they call a "pilot program" in order to build in short-term evaluation and to lower the threshold of perceived risk. Listening is one such form of regular evaluation.

At a recent pastors' conference I learned about a denominational regional body of congregations who chose to give 100 dollars to every congregation to use on a mission project for their neighborhood, and another regional body giving away over 100,000 dollars in 5,000-dollar grants awarded to applicants wanting to experiment in Christian community. In each of these cases, the recipients of the grant are asked to determine a time for their project and then to evaluate it when that time is completed. Some terrific projects, such as a neighborhood ice cream festival, a center for message and healing arts, and a free commercial-sized laundry facility in a church basement, came from these grants. Each of them was free to attempt their project without worrying about the long-range sustainability. I pulled together some artists at this event to discuss these examples and we saw an interesting parallel to the artistic process. We noticed that artists are okay with discovering new things about themselves, a medium, or an approach through failed projects.

There are many rosy portrayals of the spiritual life that promise a life free from pain or loss. But artists who are listening often have to accept pain and loss along the way.

William Faulkner has famously advised the careful author to "kill your darlings," leaving those things that do not reintegrate to die on the editing floor. What Faulkner knew was that our most favorite ideas may prove to be only that, *our* most favorites, and that many works of art are made stronger when more objective critique is heeded. While the spiritual practice of listening (to God, to the other) can provide the inspiration to stay creative, it can also build the confidence necessary to let unsustainable projects or creative missteps pass away.

On Ash Wednesday Christians remind each other that we come from ashes and will return to those ashes. Listening nurtures the centeredness and mutuality required to dare allow our pet projects to return to the ashes from whence they have come.

Listening to Your Life through Your Pilot Project

exercise 30

There is an ancient practice called *examen,* or the examination of conscience. At the core of this practice is a daily examination, listening to your life. In this exercise you'll take your forty-day pilot project and ask some questions about its role within your life and your medium. For the remainder of your forty-day practice, set aside ten minutes at the beginning and end of your day to reflect on one of these questions:

Begin by being still. For about a minute, notice your breathing and let your mind rest.

1. Listen to your life. Where do you expect to (or did you) feel alive today? Where do you expect to (or did you) feel drained or withdrawn?

2. Listen to your medium. Think of your list of materials, or people who are part of your craft. Like sculptor Andy Goldsworthy described the process of getting to know the stones, how does your work grow "in proportion

to [your] understanding"? What do you expect (or did you find) to be the most challenging today? What did you expect (or did you find) to be the easiest part today? What did you discover about your art, your community, your calling today?

Conclude the exercise by letting go of these observations: As we learn from Jesus' multiple parables about stewardship of resources or talents, there is a thin line between squandering talents and being owned by them. At the end of the day, after noticing how you or your mediums met or missed your expectations, or noting surprises along the way, let go of those things. Like a parent tucking in a child or a pastor giving a benediction, put your observations to rest where they can grow and mature outside of your conscious control.

(Wave 5 of 6)

Reintegration: joining ourselves to God's creative project

In our Atlanta neighborhood of 1910 bungalows, there are few driveways, so many of us park along the street. Nearby is a very active church attended mostly by people who commute from other parts of town, filling up the streets for blocks.

A friend of mine lives right across the street from this church and he tells of one Christmas morning when he was carefully marking spaces off for a family brunch and a church member tried to back over him into a parking space. He told the woman that his wife's grandmother would be arriving soon and they'd need the space for her, to which the church guest replied, "I didn't know you could save spaces on the public street!" He continued, explaining that the grandmother had difficulty walking and really needed a space nearby. The woman answered, "Well, this once I won't make a big deal of it! Since it's Christmas."

Granted, this is just one petty example of the confused relationships that we sometimes have with the wider creative work of God, but two-thousand-some years after those nativity angels met the shepherds with tidings of good news of great joy for all people, many of us still confuse church access for the good news.

Christianity moved into a religion of the state way back in the fourth century and it has generally enjoyed that privilege all the way up until this past century. Like that woman who felt entitled to a parking space on Christmas, we grow accustomed to thinking that we need or deserve position, privilege, or power. So much exposure and power can actually inhibit the fruit that is supposed to grow from those gathering in the power of the Spirit for the good of all creation.

Our Creator does not hide one part of creation from everything else, or keep some as an insider secret. Like a proud painter, God introduces God's apprentices to the public as both participant in God's unfolding creation and as witness to the grand creative dream.

In 1986 a couple of University of Georgia business school graduates with talent in dance jumped out on a dream: to teach modern dance to girls at the Stewart Avenue Women's Shelter in Atlanta. Dana Lupton and Leah Mann taught the inner-city girls to express their trauma and find their voice through their bodies. The girls, and the group eventually included boys as well, would learn about themselves through dance. Moving in the Spirit (MITS) would grow into a program serving children ages three to eighteen, linking support resources, mentorship, and leadership accountability to weekly class participation. Their apprentice corporation has performed before audiences in Paris and at the White House. The program has grown to include over three hundred students, 80 percent of which are on full scholarship, and 60 percent of their staff are graduates of their program.

"If you strip the dance away, it's about young people finding their voice," Lupton says. "I want them to be agents of social change. It's about, 'What do you believe in? What are you willing to fight for?'"[115] Lupton's design for the MITS program is one of continually handing the work back to the student, reintegrating the art with the larger story.

I attended MITS's latest original performance, *Between Worlds*, at Georgia State's Rialto Theater and sat amazed at the expressiveness of the dancers and the skill of their performance. Some of the performers were kids I had known and watched develop for ten years. The narration written by poet Alice Lovelace was woven from the stories she had culled from interviews with the student dancers and ancient origin stories. The choreography was designed by the dancers themselves, as participants in the story. Lovelace said that "in the end they're dancing to their own stories."[116]

But the program requires Lupton, Lovelace, and the dozen instructors to place the art beyond themselves, returning the beauty to the world. Even enrollment depends on the free choice of the students. Lupton confesses, "They have to come to us. . . . We can't go find them once they disappear. Together we can be strong, but when you lose them it's just heartbreaking."[117]

God's creative work returns full circle until "God gathers all things trembling to himself."[118] And so, while everything is freely given, nothing turns up wasted—even God's glory and power. In the final chapter of the first book of Chronicles, we read about King David handing down his kingdom to his son Solomon at the dedication of the temple materials. His dedication prayer included:

> Yours, O LORD, are the greatness, the power, the glory, the victory, and the majesty . . . yours is the kingdom. . . . In your hand are power and might; and it is in your hand to make great and to give strength to all. . . . All things come from you, and of your own have we given you. For we are aliens and transients before you, as were all our ancestors, our days on the earth are like a shadow, and there is no hope. O LORD our God, all this abundance that we have provided for building you a house for your holy name comes from your hand and is all your own. (1 Chronicles 29:11–16 NRSV)

In the same way that we say at a funeral that ashes return to ashes and dust to dust, the artisans being given over three hundred tons of gold and six hundred tons of silver to build the temple knew that all those materials were in process as part of God's creative handiwork. Any commissioned artisan, after building the installation, must eventually leave it to the world to work with.

Jesus referenced David's commissioning prayer in the conclusion to the prayer he gave to his disciples. Jesus knew that the stuff, time, and footprints that we utilize to accomplish our work all pour from the Creator's own creative hand. In the rhythms of the spiritually creative life, completed work is finally returned to the world from which we've borrowed it. We don't need to clamor for glory or power or reign, it is God's to freely share, and God desires that all will taste and see this glory, power, and reign. Paul would explain it this way:

> I pray that you, being rooted and established in love, may have power, together with all the Lord's holy people, to grasp how wide and long and high and deep is the love of Christ, and to know this love that surpasses knowledge—that you may be filled to the measure of all the fullness of God.

Now to him who is able to do immeasurably more than all we ask or imagine, according to his power that is at work within us, to him be glory in the church and in Christ Jesus throughout all generations, for ever and ever! Amen. (Ephesians 3:17–21 NIV)

We live in a time of great fragmentation. We separate our income from our pleasure. We separate our friends from our neighbors. We separate church from vacation, work from play, savings from expenses. We can segment our media by genre and egocast only the music and news we want to hear. In such an age, Paul's prayer seems pertinent, that we would know a larger integrative whole, an all-surpassing love. The rhythm of reintegration is entrusting the materials that we make, the time we invest, and the limited power and glory we hold to the larger whole of God's dreams. We return our artwork to the larger commission.

Community organizer and systems guru Margaret J. Wheatley observes how power flows through organizations. Drawing from quantum physics that assumes that all atoms are interconnected, she suggests that various organizations' ways of behaving can generate negative or positive charges to their power based on the type of relationships. "When power is shared in such workplace redesigns as participative management and self managed teams, positive creative power abounds," experienced as high productivity or job satisfaction. While in workplaces where "leaders attempt to force better results through coercion and competition" the energy is "entirely negative." In such cases, she writes, "power becomes a problem, not a capacity." Her conclusion is this:

If power is generated by our relationships, then we need to be attending to the *quality* of those relationships. We would do well to ponder the realization that love is the most potent source of power.[119]

Beyond all we can ask or imagine is God's love drawing all things to God's self. And so the nature of our connection to all those things is worth investigating.

The phrase "You are God's workmanship created in Christ Jesus" is couched by Paul in a larger conversation about fragmentation. He wrote that Jews and the Gentile Ephesians—labeled by some Jewish Christ-followers as infidels—no longer needed to see the world in that insider/outsider way. They (and we) are all connected, all building blocks in a new temple, a living temple where God dwells. God's character marks every tribe and family; God destines us to be together as one body.

So how do we—artists who feel certain commitments to the way of Christ—relate to the rest of the world in which we live?

Do we set our work into conversation with the world around us, or hide it in places where it cannot be seen? Do we expand our own vision of our work by learning from and appreciating arts that are not our own, that were not our ideas, that do not benefit our causes?

One mission scholar has said that the church is the "hermeneutic of the gospel."[120] This is to say, the good news is read by others as they encounter Jesus' followers collaboratively creating. Another scholar on church and mission has suggested that the church "is not the end user of the gospel."[121] Both of these phrases have implications with regard to the intentional coordination of creative work and the drawing in of others to that work.

How much of what you create is designed to give back to the universe from which it came? The material stuff we make is no different than the ingredients of our flesh and bones. Water, carbon, gas. Ashes to ashes, dust to dust. What good is it to hoard up moments, footprints, and stuff here on earth where moths and rust nibble them back into dust?

Like the Native American gift of the peace pipe, our gifts belong to the whole. This plays out in everything from church-based urban development to various approaches to congregational worship. In some approaches to urban ministry, churches move into an at-risk neighborhood with an expectation that their changes will be welcomed fixes to what they see as pain or loss in that community. But as participants in the gift of God's continuing creation, we must also participate as fellow citizens, learning from one another.

Theologian Ed Farley writes, "Drawn into the empathetic life with the other, the human being then praises God, experiences the divine presence, and contemplates divine mysteries." But without what Farley calls "ethical self-transcendence," worship and praise (ranging from the most traditional to the most contemporary) "remain instances of natural egocentrism and even idolatrous self-securing."[122] The creative life in the way of Jesus—and by extension, the work of church formation—is rooted in God's beauty revealed through others and experienced in our friendship with others.

There is an old Gaelic folk legend of a magical cow that would fill any vessel with milk, no matter the size or shape. Her fame spread throughout the countryside. The cow's owner knew her value and so he commissioned his seven sons to continually keep watch so that one always stood next to her. One evening the son who was to be watching her fell under an enchanted sleep and a wicked woman snuck in with a sieve. She proceeded to milk the cow into the sieve, milk spilling endlessly out into the ground, until the cow was completely spent and keeled over.

In the morning when the son awoke, he saw milk pouring out in seven directions under the cow's body and he ran to get his family. When the father and sons returned, the cow was gone; she was never seen again. After some time seven streams sprung up from that place that remain a reminder to the people of the region of the importance of cherishing our limits.[123]

What kind of vessel are you? How often do you fall asleep on the watch and let someone sneak up in the night to suck limitless life out of you? Knowing your place in the world is an important way to celebrate who you are and to prepare yourself to rest. It's a discipline that, when matched to the calling to create, frees the artist to complete and awaken each new day to God's new mercies. But hoarding our gifts and creations is like trying to store manna overnight or daring the cow of abundance to prove its magic. Our gifts and creations will rot, they will eat away at the very story we are making, they will eventually vanish.

Jesus described teaching hardened hearts as being like throwing your grandmother's heirloom gem into a pigsty. If pigs mistake it as slop, they'll eat it and excrete it. If they confuse it as uncomfortable mud clumps they'll trample it into pieces. He described his contemporaries as fans begging for more flute songs and more street concerts. Like drunken frat boys at an indie show, many of those for whom we make religious art will not appreciate it for art's sake. And many of those to whom the church panders most naturally and easily would rather be validated as a consumer market (if it is purchased or consumed readily, then it must be valuable) than challenged to do the work of learning.

Jesus also told a parable about the kingdom of God being like a mythical mustard bush growing, like Jack's magic beanstalk, into a huge tree until birds of the air made nests in it. The dreams of God do not belong hidden behind church doors or institutions; they should be shared with everything and everyone. Likewise, creative exploits done in the name of the church cannot remain hidden behind internal language and symbols. The dreams of God belong "out there," integrated with the world beyond the church's doors. The artful life of the follower of God belongs in the language of the context in which they live. The dreams of God are like a mustard seed that grows magically beyond its determined DNA into something large enough to hold others, to hold birds of all feathers.

John's Revelation would describe another magical tree. Actually a pair of trees, these trees of life, would sit on either side of the mighty Life River flowing from God's own throne through the New Jerusalem. These trees are like the magical cow, bearing fruit every month, eternally. And the leaves from the trees are to be for the "healing of the nations" and not simply for the healing of the residents of the New Jerusalem. The work of God is beneficial to all, like rain falling on the just and unjust.

And so the creative work of God's commissioned artists involves sharing, generously giving what we've found to be beautiful, good, and true, with the world in which we live. We must share with no strings attached, out of mutual appreciation and curiosity. As such, reintegration is a form of letting go.

Integrating Your Work with the Work of Others
exercise 31

For the following exercise you will interview four people. Focus on one of the following contexts: your neighborhood, your church tradition, your art medium, or your personal life.

Inquire: Ask them the following (you should phrase your questions specific to the context you have chosen):

a. How long have you considered yourself a part of this community/trade (or known me)?

b. How would you tell our history (my story)?

c. When have you felt most helpful or alive in this group (or observed me most alive)?

d. When have you been most angry or afraid (or observed me as such)?

e. What physical things or places around here are most important to you (or come to mind when you think of me)?

Map: Find the best way to visualize the four stories: put the observations on sticky notes and cluster them into related groups that map the relationships; compare and contrast them using a timeline; create a Venn diagram; or create a graph with x- and y-axes to help you emphasize tensions and create different categories.[124] Pay attention to significant contextual issues (landmarks, stuff that matters, lines of influence).

Observe: Now look at your work and take note of what surprises you. Articulate your observations as open-ended statements or questions. For example: "I'm curious about the connection between . . . " or, "I wonder why she didn't say . . . "

Synthesize: As a last step, read Galatians 5:13–26 and see how God's love leads a creative person into healthy relatedness and out of selfish ambition and acquisitiveness. Visualize the dreams and risks you have taken and compare them to how "[God] brings gifts into our lives, much the same way that fruit appears in an orchard" (MSG). Returning to the four interviews, picture yourself and the other four individuals as trees in a larger orchard.

Contemplate: Journal or sketch your observations.

(Wave 6 of 6)

Rest: laying down the paintbrush

Surrender is the beginning of rest. It leads us to the still waters where we can "be still and know" that God is God.

We frequently mistake stopping for quitting. Many activists and creatives grow suspicious of inaction. We get anxious when things begin to slow. When all the outside voices subside, our internal critics and disappointment begin to scream at us. They scream at us in blame or they project blame at others around us. But silence leaves room for the encore. Silence is a gate, a doorway into rest, where the body and mind must become reacquainted. The unexamined voices that push and push us have to be acknowledged and dismissed.

One of my favorite encore stories is the ending of U2's shows in the '80s and '90s when Bono would call up a fan from the crowd and hand him a guitar to play the song "40" with the band. As the congregation sang the psalm, "How long to sing this song?" one band member after another would walk off the stage. Larry Mullen Jr. would lay down his sticks. Adam Clayton and The Edge would unplug their guitars and walk away. And Bono would throw down his mic stand and disappear backstage. U2 would be done for the night, but the song would continue as the lucky fan, having the night of his life, played away at the three chords of the song while the crowd continued to sing, "I will sing, sing a new song."

Rest is a way of surrendering to the unknown, finishing and handing off the watch to the next shift.

> What is the prayer of a heart grown calm
> > in the peace of God?
> From such a purity one no longer prays
> > as we are wont to pray.
> From such a purity one is free from asking
> > any further gift of God, and is free
> > also from asking that anything
> > be taken away.
> A heart in calm detachment asks
> > for nothing, nor has anything
> > it would wish to shed.
> Its prayer is finally only for its uniformity
> > with God. This is its entire prayer.
> —Meister Eckhart, translation by Scott Cairns[125]

Sometimes resting involves letting go of resolution, a freedom from asking for more or for less. But that leaves us vulnerable.

Thomas was one of Jesus' followers who most vulnerably confessed his need for resolution. He wasn't around on that definitive morning when the resurrected Jesus showed up to his friends. Perhaps he was walking through the streets and along the seas where Jesus had previously walked with him. Perhaps he was afraid and hiding in seclusion. Perhaps he had been on an errand while the women came from the tomb, running up to Peter and John to announce the empty tomb and their encounter with the resurrected Jesus. Whatever the case, Thomas longed for resolution. So when Jesus appeared before him in that upper room, Thomas' first response was to keep him at bay. Thomas admitted his place of unbelief, the unknown space. In response, Jesus gently showed him his hands and side.

A few years ago I spent time with that passage about Thomas for Holy Week and couldn't shake the idea that the scene between Jesus and Thomas was a sort of Sabbath image. It seemed that the usual takes on this were forced, trying to make a modern courtroom jury out of Thomas, when Thomas had been well acquainted with Jesus as his apprentice. I don't think Thomas was in that frequently preached defensive posture, or that Jesus was leveling an apologetic to his friend. Jesus did not need his disciple's validation. And Jesus didn't want Thomas to grasp some big idea. Jesus wanted his friend to let go of the struggle, and he knew that Thomas' body just needed to catch up to his mind.

Creatives can struggle with this sort of rest. It is easy to become a workaholic, leveraging every friendship into material for the novel, every picturesque moment into fodder for a future shoot. Thomas was jammed up needing an answer; meanwhile, Jesus was present with him, just as he'd hoped. Rest is that place where we can let go of the control, the search for another output, the need for validation.

But as we saw in the exercise of listening, God's vision of loving-relatedness places work into the context of relationship. As such, our shared goals and shared labor are to be understood cooperatively as well. Have you ever considered how your vision affects those who share space with you, or work for you? Have you thought of how your own body participates as a cog in the labor multiplication needed to accomplish others' goals? God's vision for your "good-working-ness" is not some mechanistic efficiency. It is one of cooperation.

Many religious, academic, and even scientific institutions offer sabbatical leave every seven years as a built-in respite for their workers. Rooted in the rhythms of God's own creative process, the Levitical law required that Hebrew farmers, their plowing animals, and the farm land all rest on the seventh year as well. Like the Sabbath day, the seventh of the week, resting on the seventh *year* was a hallowed intentional practice to reverse the affects of the endless labor Egypt had worn into the Hebrews in slavery. Today, sabbaticals are also intended to reverse the effects of seemingly endless labor. Many take the opportunity to reconnect to their partner and their children, to write or travel, to pick up a hobby or to attend to their body through exercise and holism.

But not everyone gets a sabbatical, and hardly anyone can afford to give up a year's pay every seven years. What disciplines will you invent to create your own time of rest? The monks maintain this practice in their week, with a day off of work. Many creatives find rest in planning times away from social media and TV or "artist dates" at a magazine stand, a CD store, or walking through the woods. Consider taking time to walk freely and lightly with the children in your life. Like the Pomodoro techniques of time boxing, make space for rest, make space for exercise, set date nights with your partner, make time to make love, and to enjoy a slow cup of coffee.

A couple of years ago I was introduced to the holistic practice of dietary cleansing, which taught me a lot about the connection between my body's rest and my mind's rest. My health coach helped me slowly wean myself off of the caffeine, alcohol, nicotine, carbs, and chocolate that I had been using to artificially modify my body's pace. These had been stifling my body's warnings to slow down and clouding my discernment about what else was influencing me. About four days in, after cutting out sugar and caffeine, my body went through what health coaches call a *healing crisis*. That night I was feverish, sick to my stomach, and my ears and throat ached like I had the flu. Within a few more days I was past the worst of it. After a month of all raw foods, no dairy, meat, or gluten, my eyes were whiter, my skin was brighter, my sinuses were open, and my mind was unbelievably clear. That thirty-day cleanse opened my eyes to the effects of a lifetime of ignoring my body. I can't begin to imagine the effect of the hundreds of years of tireless work the Hebrew slaves endured, or how many seventh-year sabbaticals it would take to free their minds and bodies.

Wayne Muller, founder of Bread for the Journey, writes, "When we move too fast we shield ourselves from the actual experience of suffering; we see only its outward manifestations and appearances. In our frantic craving for relief, we try to make the appearance of suffering go away. But we risk eradicating the symptoms without ever understanding the disease." On the other hand, "When we enter into a relationship with a community in need, when we sit quietly and listen, and patiently wait, a host of people with priceless gifts, talents, and strengths invariably arise."[126] At a retreat led by Muller, I was introduced to the great seven-minute sharing of "loves" (as we practiced in exercise 21) and to what he described as the sacred act of "sauntering"—slowing down one's gait until the feet and land meet as partners in a conversation.

In his *Letters to a Young Poet,* Rainer Maria Rilke describes the deep place of waiting for the birth of "new clarity." "In this there is no measuring of time," he writes, "a year doesn't matter, and ten years are nothing. Being an artist means: not numbering and counting, but ripening like the tree which does not force its sap, and stands confident in the storms of spring not afraid that summer may not come."[127]

The time to bear fruit comes, he encourages, "But it comes only to those who are patient, who are there as if eternity lay before them, so unconcernedly silent and vast."[128] Like a tree planted by streams of water bearing fruit when it's the right season, Sabbath helps return us to those streams of living water, and take our mind off of whether we're due fruit or not.

Sabbath is also that space where pain and possibility emerge, unforced, and our bodies get to do their job of working past them. On the other side is clarity and restored hope, but only for them that wait. And for Christian creatives, Sabbath rest also brings a clarity of vision and work.

From time to time, in my conversations with my Buddhist friend, Jim, I'll ask him his perspective on a theological conundrum and he'll bring his hands together and intone, "Ohhhhhm." By this, I take him to mean that he practices rather than believes. Like Rilke advises, he wants to avoid the false stimulants, shortcuts, and artificial preservatives that rationale can bring, viewing the world instead from the vantage point of practice, from embodiment.

Could Jesus and Thomas' encounter over belief have been a similar gesture? Could it have been less of an argument over the possibility of resurrection and more of a poetic living into the unsolved places, a surrendering and resting of argumentation? I think that Jesus could have been inviting Thomas out of his head and into his whole body: "Put your finger here; see my hands. Reach out your hand and put it into my side. Stop doubting and believe" (John 20:27 NIV). Note the careful connection between Jesus' hands and Thomas'.

Sabbath is that space where we quit taking shortcuts, quit making strategies, we even quit pushing for the prize. Instead, we let our whole selves enter into the present so that new convictions can emerge.

A practice that Jim taught me is one he calls direct experience. Take a cup of coffee or tea. Sit with it without assuming it will be what you have touched countless times in the past. Notice the feel of the mug against your fingers: is it coarse, smooth, hot, cold, wet, dry? Now smell the aromas. Do you notice other smells, such as chocolate, lemon, caramel, the fresh smell of cut grass? As you raise the cup to your mouth, note the wrinkles in your lips and the rises that touch the mug first. Ask yourself, what name would I give to this cup, and what is in it? Perhaps the Hebrew word *manna*, "What is it?" and the Hebrew prohibition against writing or speaking the name of God are such a hallowing of those mysterious unknown spaces in our life.

The discipline of direct experience can teach the artist to notice that much of life is in a perpetual state of change, and that we can remain learners in regard to who we believe ourselves and others to be.

In Israel, at the end of seven sabbaticals, so at forty-nine years, Levitical law called for a year of Jubilee, an ultimate form of Sabbath (Leviticus 25:8–55). Scholars have argued whether it was ever practiced, but the vision was of an entire year during which all construction was suspended, indentured debtors were freed, debt was reset to zero, and property was returned to the early tribes. Jubilee was designed to halt the race after bigger and better. Yet, God's secession of making was not a condemnation of making. It was establishing a rhythm, a monastic habit, an art to living. And the cycle does not end with stopping. When we are well rested we are able, once again, to dream.

Inspiration comes to those that wait. Often one problem leads to another, and so Sabbath is that speed bump to bring the creative back full circle to a place of dreaming. Mihaly Csikszentmihalyi noted in his list of ten traits of the creative personality that "creative people have a great deal of physical energy, but they're also often quiet and at rest." Archimedes was said to have discovered the principal of buoyancy while bathing. Leonardo da Vinci has written, "It is . . . a good plan every now and then to go away and have a little relaxation, for then, when you come back to the work, your judgment will be surer, since to remain constantly at work causes you to lose the power of judgment."[129]

One of Alfred Hitchcock's actors, Hume Cronyn, tells of a time when Hitchcock showed him how to stop. "One time, we were working on a problem with a scene. There were a lot of things to consider—lighting, staging, pacing, and the like. We were up very late struggling to find the right way to do it. Finally, when we seemed close to the solution, Hitchcock came in and started telling jokes, silly junior high–type stuff and got us all lost again. Later I asked him why, when we were so close to solving the problem, did he choose that moment to get us off track by joking around? He paused and said something I'll never forget. He said, 'You were pushing. It never comes from pushing.'"[130]

Sabbath is that laughter. It is that place where we don't reckon or count. It is a place of abundance; a place of vulnerable trust; a full body embrace; a cleansing, inhaling, opening rest from pushing. The creative life we are created to live can never come from pushing. It happens when we give up on striving and are drawn in.

And when we've rested well, we begin to dream once again. So the cycle continues and continues, as the dreams of God unfold and expand until all things are made new.

Planning Sabbath, Setting the Stage for Future Dreams   exercise 32

My friend Mark Scandrette has beautifully articulated the cyclical rhythms of spiritual practices. "The goal of shared practices is to become fully alive to the power that is making all things new. . . . In the spiritual realm as in the scientific, experiments lead to more questions that beget further experiments, just as reaching the top of one vista reveals the path upward toward another, more beautiful view further up and further in."[131]

As we've seen, the process of creating leads full circle from planning to making to letting go and then back again. In your creative life you will travel countless times through the rhythms of dreaming, hovering, risking, listening, integrating, and resting. So the challenge in taking responsibility for the studio of your life is the tension between forcing or discovering that rhythm. Most of us aren't people who can unplug from our jobs and move into a monastery. But we have to plan to stop if we are truly to discover the restoring power of rest.

Take a look at your calendar for the next year. Can you afford a time away to a place of restoration? What kind of budgeting will you need to do to be ready for that? Can you make a place to be careless and to play? Place speed bumps in your calendar: times of vacation with loved ones, times to exercise, days to sleep in, date nights, and retreats to dig in to your craft or underexplored writing and creative desires. Once you have set several dates of different sorts, write yourself a short note about this creative process. Note the letting go and resting necessary to continue dreaming and risking. Write your note on a card and revisit it during these various Sabbaths. Share your dates with a friend or loved one and invite them to possibly reserve the dates as well, as a sort of relational contract. Your calling is born out of the unforced places and is nurtured in those moments as well.

What's Next?

Jesus spent three years demonstrating that he and the Father are one as he reintroduced us to the art of creation in the life of God.

At the end of those three years, on the cross of Roman capital punishment, when Jesus gasped, "Forgive them," he was saying to God that the dance must continue and that those he longed to commune with require forgiveness to stay in that dance.

Now, as his apprentices, our gasps should be no different. We, like Peter, find our true callings when we let go of our attempts to protect God and allow God to make us into cocreators.

Jesus' risk, taking on flesh, dying on the cross, and entering into new life blows open the vision and expands the work of God's calling to all of us as artists. The sacramental curtain is torn and a halo is widened to orbit all things. The dividing barrier between us and God, and between individuals, is gone. It's not that humanity's history as a people relating to God up to that point is invalidated, it's that our vantage point on history has expanded. And as a person's relatedness to God and humanity's consciousness of God expands, we are further invited into and equipped for the creative dance of life.

One of my old seminary professors, Darrell Guder, has suggested that the church is "continually undergoing conversion" as we are regularly reintroduced to the challenging vision of God's kingdom.[132] In doing so, we also and always need to regularly change our postures. The language in Isaiah of trees joining in applause, of deserts bursting with rivers, of lions and lambs living side by side, the ancient hymn quoted in Philippians about every knee and every tongue participating—all these images and more might inspire us to *imagineer* more and more ways for God's dreams to be realized.

Like Buckminster Fuller, who designed bridges that required yet-to-be-discovered technology, we can build anticipatory lives. We can create beauty and rest in the freedom that we are part of generations of apprentices working on God's visions. So, even if we don't currently have the technology for it, our life can lead to the technology we'll require.

Can we get drawn in by picking up the crayon, by collaborating with wider and wider groups of artists, and by making those things that are larger than us—bigger than our own selves? Simply put, yes!

You are God's works of art created in Christ Jesus to be working parts of the very art as it unfolds. So jump in.

The experience of art has shown me that creation does not happen in a vacuum. Art is cultivated within a creative environment. As far back as I can remember, people around me have been nudging me to create. Even my first guitar was a gift from friends and mentors determined that my cheapness or fear of failure not squelch that deepest draw to create.

I'm energized by recounting all the generous support folks have given along the way to bringing this book into reality. The germ for this book came from my first year in seminary when I studied the "Preacher and the Poet" with Anna Carter Florence, missiology with Darrell Guder, and then worked to develop a theological conversation between my professor Walter Brueggemann and the newly formed Emergent Village. Then, in my last semester in seminary, Rick Dietrich introduced our small class of would-be-preachers to aesthetics. We studied many of the books that would become sources for this one, and he planted a little seed by saying, "I didn't want you all to finish your years in seminary hearing that God could only be spoken of in terms of power or dogma." This opened a horizon for me where beauty and faith intermingled.

The actual book has been cobbled together thanks to half a dozen barrowed studies and get-aways. Around 2008 Doug Pagitt and Carla Barnhill gave me a few frozen days of their Minneapolis winter to sort through the beginnings of this book. In the Fall of 2009 I spent two weeks writing in an empty Sunday school room at College Park Presbyterian, thanks to the support of Jay

Thomas. Later the next Spring I did the same at Ryan Gravel's family cabin in Gunnersville, Alabama. Then in the Summer of 2010 I spent several months writing weekly at a cubicle amidst the creative staff of Buckhead Church Atlanta, thanks to the support of John Hambrick. By the time Paraclete Press got behind the project, my friend and neighbor Derek Koehl was my first editor, and then Jon Sweeny, with Paraclete, walked with me the rest of the way. The Paraclete staff has been incredible with countless approaches to cover design, crediting and indexing, marketing, and web support. Jason Orme, Jonathan Stegall, and Travis Eckmark have given countless hours to the web site and Paul Soupiset has done amazing work on the supportive art materials for the web.

I want to thank the congregation of Neighbors Abbey who helped me take risks to intentionally follow Jesus in innercity Atlanta, and the congregation of City Church Eastside who gave expression to beauty and indigenous worship far beyond my wildest imagination! Special thanks to my new congregational family, Northminster Presbyterian Church in Cincinnati, Ohio. I look forward to the years of being drawn in together to God's work as I serve as curator with the artists there.

I most want to thank my wife Kelley and our kids, Eve and Wakefield, for sharing me with so many creatives and Jesus followers over the years, learning these stories and honing these insights into something that I hope will inspire the creativity of many to come. I dedicate this first book to the great risk-taking that my wife has taken in building a life with a creative. May my readers know the joy found in such deeply generative relationships that challenge and fund their own life's art. Thank you, Kelley!

1   Scott Cairns, *Love's Immensity: Mystics on the Endless Life* (Brewster, MA: Paraclete Press, 2007), 61. I am indebted to Cairns for the soul-care that engendered much of this book, and especially for these poems. Several of his poetic translations of the patristics, mystics, and desert ammas and abbas will appear in the pages to follow.

2   Chaim Potok, *My Name Is Asher Lev* (New York: A. A. Knopf, 1975), 304.

3   Madeleine L'Engle, *Walking on Water: Reflections on Faith and Art* (Colorado Springs, CO: Shaw, 2001), 72.

4   Darrell Guder, *The Incarnation and the Church's Witness* (Harrisburg, PA: Trinity Press International, 1999), 3.

5   I have changed the names of several of the individuals in this book at their requests, in order to protect their identity and yet honor their stories.

6   Gregory Wolfe, "Liturgical Arts and Its Discontents," in *Intruding Upon the Timeless: Meditations on Art, Faith, and Mystery* (Baltimore: Square Halo Press, 2003), 91, 92.

7   From Emmylou Harris's song "O Evangeline," found in *Stumble into Grace* (Nonesuch Records, 2003). Also from Matthew 11:28–30 MSG.

8   Thomas Merton, *Contemplative Prayer* (New York: Doubleday, 1971), 13.

9   Ellen Lupton, ed., *D.I.Y.: Design It Yourself* (New York: Princeton Architectural Press, 2006), 31.

10 Ibid. "Organic Intellectuals" is a reference to the work of Antonio Gramsci.

11 In 2011, while I was wrapping up this manuscript, three outstanding books emerged addressing the church's relationship with worship arts and arts in general, and I commend them all to you: Jonny Baker, ed., *Curating Worship* (New York: Seabury, 2011); W. David O. Taylor, ed., *For the Beauty of the Church: Casting a Vision for the Arts* (Grand Rapids, MI: Baker Books, 2010); and Mark Pierson, *The Art of Curating Worship: Reshaping the Role of Worship Leader* (Minneapolis: Sparkhouse Press, 2010).

12 Jeremy Begbie's writing first suggested this acoustic metaphor to me. See Begbie's "Through Music," in *Beholding the Glory:*

Incarnation Through the Arts (Grand Rapids, MI: Baker Books, 2001), 144 *ff*.

13   I'm indebted to the thorough summary and hypothesis of Edward Farley in *Faith and Beauty: A Theological Aesthetic*. (Burlington, VT: Ashgate Publishing Company, 2001) for the concept of "self-transcending benevolence."

14   Vincent van Gogh, *The Complete Letters of Vincent Van Gough* (Boston: New York Graphics Society, 1978), B 9, II, 499. I'm grateful to the work of Don Postema's *Space for God: The Study and Practice of Prayer and Spirituality* (Grand Rapids, MI: Board of Publications of the Christian Reformed Church, 1983) for this reference and for some of my earliest notions about God as artist.

15   Much of my work leading to the six-part process is a synthesis of personal work, biblical study, and from work of systems psychologists and emerging practices design thinking. See Mihaly Csikszentmihalyi, *Creativity: Flow and the Psychology of Discovery and Invention* (New York: Harper Perennial, 1996). Also, check out design thinking as taught by IDEO or Stanford school of design. Teachers and pastors should visit http://www.designthinkingforeducators.com.

16   R. Buckminster Fuller and Kiyoshi Kuromiya, *Cosmography: A Posthumous Scenario for the Future of Humanity* (New York: MacMillan, 1992), 52.

17   There are numerous approaches to this eschatological notion of God's loving future-oriented design. N. T. Wright has written that "what God did for Jesus at Easter he will do . . . for the entire cosmos" (*Surprised By Hope* [New York: Harper Collins, 2008], 99). And earlier, Jürgen Moltmann's *Theology of Hope* is built upon the premise that "Hope statements of promise anticipate a future. In the promises, the hidden future already announces itself and exerts its influence on the present through the hope it awakens" (Moltmann, *Theology of Hope* [Minneapolis: Fortress Press, 1993], 18–19). And Thomas Merton has written, "To say that I am made in the image of God is to say that love is the reason for my existence, for God is love. Love is my true identity. . . . The root of Christian love is not the will to love, but the faith that one is loved . . . by God" (Merton, *New Seeds of Contemplation* [New York: New Directions, 2007], 60, 75).

18   You can learn more about Todd Fadell's music and musings at www.loveisconcrete.ning.com.

19   The KJV translates this as Voice, others as sound of God. Each emphasize the location of God's material resonance in the garden *with* Adam and Eve. An interesting parallel is drawn between *voice* and the *vocation* of the person in Parker Palmer's *Let Your Life Speak: Listening for the Voice of Vocation* (San Francisco: Jossey-Bass, 2000).

20   Origen of Alexandria, in Cairns, *Love's Immensity*, 12.

21   Wayne Muller, *Sabbath: Finding Rest, Renewal, and Delight in Our Busy Lives* (New York: Bantam, 1999), 82–83.

22   Philippians 4:6–7; "prayer and supplication with thanksgiving" is from kjv; "sense of God's wholeness" is from Peterson's *The Message.*

23   Henri Nouwen, "Moving from Solitude to Community," Leadership Journal, Spring 1995, http:/www.christianitytoday.com/le/1995/spring/51280.html.

24   Fyodor Dostoevsky, *The Brothers Karamazov* (London: Wordsworth Editions, 2007), 352, 353.

25   Everett Fox, ed., *The Five Books of Moses: Genesis, Exodus, Leviticus, Numbers, Deuteronomy* (New York: Schocken Books, 1995), 271.

26   "History" from Wendell Berry, *The Selected Poems of Wendell Berry* (Berkley, CA: Counterpoint, 1998), 101.

27   Ibid.

28   N. T. Wright, *Surprised By Hope: Rethinking Heaven, the Resurrection, and the Mission of the Church* (New York: Harper Collins, 2008), 68.

29   Eberhard Arnold, *When the Time Was Fulfilled: On Advent and Christmas* (Rifton, NY: Plough Publishing House, 1965). Arnold (1883–1935) was a German Christian writer, philosopher, and theologian. He founded the Bruderhof Communities in 1920.

30   See Claus Otto Scharmer, *Theory U: Leading from the Emerging Future* (Cambridge, MA: Society for Organizational Learning, 2007) and Peter Senge, et al., *Presence: Human Purpose and the Field of the Future* (Cambridge, MA: SoL, 2004).

31   Scharmer, Theory U executive summary can be found at http://www.ottoscharmer.com/publications/summaries.php.

32   John Geirland, "Go with the Flow," *Wired*, September 1996, http://www.wired.com/wired/archive/4.09/czik_pr.html.

33   Walter Brueggemann, *Hopeful Imagination: Prophetic Voices in Exile* (Philadelphia: Fortress Press, 1986), 56–57.

34   Learn more about the Cirillo's Pomodoro Technique at www.pomodorotechnique.com. The site is filled with many free resources.

35   Emmylou Harris, "Here I Am," *Stumble Into Grace* (Nonesuch, 2003).

36   K. L. Spalding, R. D. Bhardwaj, B. A. Buchholz, H. Druid, J. Frisen, "Retrospective Birth Dating of Cells in Humans," *Cell* 122:133–43. Also see Nicholas Wade, "Your Body Is Younger Than You Think," *New York Times,* August 2, 2005. This article contains some additional information about the life spans of different tissues that isn't discussed in the paper by Spalding et al.

37   Thomas Merton, *No Man Is an Island* (Boston: Shambhala, 2005), xxi. First published in 1955 by Our Lady of Gethsemani.

38   Attributed to Michelangelo di Lodovico Buonarroti Simoni (1475–1564), Italian Renaissance painter, sculptor, poet, engineer.

39   Elizabeth Barrett Browning, "Aurora Leigh, Book VII," *The Complete Poetical Works of Elizabeth Barrett Browning* (Whitefish, MT: Kessingers Publishing, 2005), 134.

40   Potok, *My Name Is Asher Lev,* 212.

41   Jürgen Moltmann, *In the End, the Beginning: The Life of Hope* (Minneapolis: Augsburg Fortress, 2004), 41.

42   Palmer, *Let Your Life Speak,* 10.

43   Bill Knott is an avant-garde poet and prose author of over ten books. This poem, "To Myself," is from his free self-published works found on his website: http://billknottpoetry.blogspot.com.

44   Rainer Maria Rilke, letter to Clara Rilke, Oct. 21, 1907, from *Letters on Cézanne,* ed. Clara Rilke (New York: North Point Press, 2002), 66.

45   Lewis Hyde, *The Gift: Creativity and the Artist in the Modern World* (New York: Random House Vintage Books, 2007), xii, 43. Throughout the book Hyde uses metaphors ranging from the Native American's Potlatch, to organ dontation, to Frued's annalysis of a mother's relationship with a child to illustrate how gifts entail donation.

46   Walter Brueggemann writes in *The Prophetic Imagination* that such imagery criticizes and energizes a break from both triumphalism and oppression. Walter Brueggeman, *The Prophetic Imagination* (Minneapolis: Augsburg Fortress Press, 2001), 19.

47   Otto Scharmer, interview by Peter Zak. Available at http://www.youtube.com/watch?v=k8HKxvKVUsU.

48   Elaine Scarry, *On Beauty and Being Just* (Princeton, NJ: Princeton University Press, 1999), 7.

49   Dostoyevsky, *Brothers Karamazov,* 339.

50   See the "Confession of 1967," from *The Constitution of the Presbyterian Church of the United States of America,* www.creeds.net/reformed/confess67.pdf.

51   Walter Brueggemann, from a presentation he gave at New York Avenue Presbyterian Church in Washington, DC, in 2006. Initially retrieved at http://www.nyapc.org, reprinted with permission from the author.

52   Walter Brueggemann, *Finally Comes the Poet: Daring Speech for Proclamation* (Minneapolis: Fortress Press, 1989), 6, 7.

53   Peter Rollins, *The Orthodox Heretic and Other Impossible Tales* (Brewster, MA: Paraclete Press, 2009), xi.

54   Ibid.

55   Trevor Hart, "Through the Arts: Seeing, Hearing, and Touching the Truth," in *Beholding the Glory: Incarnation Through the Arts,* ed. Jeremy Begbie (Grand Rapids, MI: Baker Books, 2000), 5 [emphasis mine].

56   Malcolm-Jamal Warner, on *The Mark Twain Prize 2009*, PBS, November 3, 2009. Video is available at http://video.pbs.org/video/1317746583.

57   Nicholas Lash, *Theology on the Way to Emmaus* (London, England: SCM Press, 1986), 41.

58   Nancy Chinn, *Spaces for Spirit: Adorning the Church* (Chicago: Liturgy Training Publications, 1998), 6, 7.

59   *a la* Brueggemann and Rollins—see n. 52 and n. 53.

60   Hart, "Through the Arts," 5.

61   Nicene Creed, 325 AD.

62   Hart, "Through the Arts," 24.

63   Jürgen Moltmann, "The Crucified God," *Theology Today* 31, no. 1 (1974): 18.

64   Dietrich Bonhoeffer, *Letters and Papers from Prison* (New York: Macmillan, 1967), 282.

65   Elizabeth O'Connor, *The Eighth Day of Creation: Gifts and Creativity* (Waco, TX: Word Books, 1971), 8.

66   Daniel Graves, quoted in Tiffany Silverman, "The Code of Apprenticeship," *Domain Magazine,* December 9, 2006.

67   *Surprise* and *interest* are related to our schemas, which the Heath brothers, Chip and Dan, describe as the "guessing machine." When an idea breaks our guessing machine, it is more likely to stick with the us. Chip Heath and Dan Heath, *Made to Stick: Why Some Ideas Survive and Others Die* (New York: Random House, 2007), 67.

68   Cairns, *Love's Immensity*, 4.

69   Lucia Capachionne, *Visioning: Ten Steps to Designing the Life of Your Dreams* (New York: J. P. Tarcher/Putman, 2000), 5.

70   Dan Roam, *The Back of the Napkin: Solving Problems and Selling Ideas with Pictures* (New York: Penguin, 2008), 4.

71   Garrett Green, *Imagining God: Theology and the Religious Imagination* (Grand Rapids, MI: Wm. B. Eerdmans, 1989), 40. Green writes: "The concept of imagination offers theology a means for resolving the dilemma of 'natural theology' or 'positivism of revelation.' Describing the point of divine-human contact in terms of imagination allows theology to do justice to both aspects of revelation: (1) as a divine act of grace, reducible to no human ability, attribute, or need, and (2) as a human act of faith, comparable in significant respects ot other forms of human experience."

72   Moltmann, "The Crucified God," 18.

73   James K. A. Smith, *Desiring the Kingdom: Worship, Worldview, and Cultural Formation* (Grand Rapids, MI: Baker Academic, 2009), 75, 80.

74   See Walter Brueggemann, *Deep Memory, Exuberant Hope: Contested Truth in a Post-Christian World* (Minneapolis: Fortress Press, 2000) and *Cadences of Home: Preaching Among Exiles* (Louisville: Westminster John Knox Press, 1997).

75   Richard Rohr, *Falling Upward: A Spirituality for the Two Halves of Life* (San Francisco: Jossey-Bass, 2011), 138.

76   Ibid, 145. See the chapter "New Problems and New Directions."

77   Nicholas Herman, *The Practice of the Presence of God and the Spiriual Maxims* (New York: Cosimo Books, 2006), 16. First published in 1895.

78   Crockett Johnson, *Harold and the Purple Crayon* (San Francisco: Harper & Row, 1955).

79   Daniel Pink, *A Whole New Mind: Why Right-Brainers Will Rule the Future* (New York: Penguin, 2005), 188. See also James Paul McGee, *What Video Games Have to Teach Us About Learning and Literacy* (New York: Palgrave Macmillan, 2003) and Doug Pagitt, *The Church in the Inventive Age* (Minneapolis: Sparkhouse Press, 2010).

80   Experts differ on whether "Wisdom" is a name for God, a reference to the Holy Spirit (a feminine voice in the Trinity), or a reference to the Son (the *logos* before being made flesh). It is beyond the scope of this book to explore all these intricacies.

81   Proverbs 8:30–31. This is my own translation based on Moltmann's suggestion that the Hebrew here for "rejoicing" could be translated "playing." Jürgen Moltmann, *Theology Play*, trans. Reinhard Ulrich (New York: Harper and Row, 1971), 40.

82   Ellen Davis, interview by Krista Tippet, *Speaking of Faith,* APM, June 10, 2010. Transcript available at http://speakingoffaith.publicradio.org/programs/2010/land-life-poetry/transcript.shtml.

83   Jürgen Moltmann, *Theology and Joy* (London: SCM Press, 1973), 62.

84   Dostoyevsky, *Brothers Karamazov,* 191, 244, 428, 829.

85   Peter Senge et al., *Presence: Human Purpose and the Field of the Future* (New York: Doubleday, 2004), 9.

86   John McKnight and Peter Block, *The Abundant Community: Awakening the Power of Families and Neighborhoods* (San Francisco: Berrett-Koehler Publishers, 2010), 78.

87   Ross Talarico, *Spreading the Word: Poetry and the Survival of Community in America* (Durham, NC: Duke University Press, 1995), 51. Talarico writes, "*Deliteracy* indicates a general lack of interest in self-expression through language and indeed a disinterest in forming perspectives. How

does it come about? *It comes from the successful misuse of language!* The culture rewards those who use language to deceive others, and abandons those who use it in attempts to enlighten."

88   Davis, interview by Krista Tippet.

89   Ibid.

90   Hyde, *The Gift*, 21, 31.

91   St. Athanasios, "His Image Recovered," in *Love's Immensity*, 15.

92   This is a phrase used throughout Peter Block's *Community: The Structure of Belonging* (San Francisco: Berrett-Koehler Publishers, 2008).

93   I am aware that talk of creation's influence on God is wading into contested theological territory. A lot of theological gymnastics have gone into explaining that God's power and authority has no strings connected to mortals, and that God only "appears" to be affected due to our limited visibility or poor resolution. First, let me say, I celebrate that much of this theology has been elegantly articulated by our foreparents in an effort to hallow God's name, honoring God's unique "All-in-All" character vis-à-vis a subjective created universe. If that is where you come from, I ask you to hang in with me by considering two things: First, might God's purpose behind "appearing" to be drawn in by our work be enough to support my point? Similar to the example God sets by resting on the seventh day, might God be demonstrating God's integrative, relational intentions of the universe that God is creating and into which we are sent? Second, if you'll recall from the last chapter, incarnational theology emphasizes that Jesus did not "appear" or seem to be human and material, but was fully located and contextual. Can you consider that the dance drawing in both us and God is a very part of God's relational DNA, and that Jesus is not, then, a momentary suspension of God's otherwise immaterial character but a unique, once-and-for-all demonstration of the relational God's loving creative decision to join creation?

94   Quote taken from Byrne's journal at http://journal.davidbyrne.com/ webtech. You can also watch Byrne's TED talk on the same matter, "How Architecture Helped Music Evolve," at http://www.ted.com/talks/david _byrne_how_architecture_helped_music_evolve.html.

95   George MacDonald, *Diary of an Old Soul: 366 Writings for Devotional Reflection* (Minneapolis: Augsburg, 1996), 30.

96   Block, *Community*, 35.

97   Ibid., 178.

98   Dallas Willard, *The Divine Conspiracy: Rediscovering Our Hidden Life in God* (San Francisco: HarperSanFrancisco, 1998), 376, 378.

99 This is Dallas Willard's paraphrase of Isaiah 65:17 and 66:18–23, in *Divine Conspiracy*, 380.

100 Marjorie J. Thompson, *Soul Feast: An Invitation to the Christian Spiritual Life* (Louisville: Westminster John Knox Press, 2005), 150.

101 Csikszentmihalyi, *Creativity*, 98.

102 Donald Campbell, quoted in Csikszentmihalyi, *Creativity*, 99.

103 Brian Eno, in *Here Is What Is*, Daniel Lanois (Red Floor Productions, 2007). Available for digital download at https://www.e-junkie.com/ecom / gb.php?c=cart&i=148203&cl=10283&ejc=2.

104 Abraham Joshua Heschel, interview by Frank Reynolds, *Directions*, ABC, November 1971. The transcript from the interview is available from the website of APM's episode of *On Being*, "The Spiritual Audacity of Abraham Joshua Heschel": http://being.publicradio.org/programs/heschel /particulars.shtml.

105 Edwin Friedman, *A Failure of Nerve: Leadership in the Age of the Quick Fix* (New York: Seabury Books, 1999), 31.

106 E. B. White, quoted in Israel Shenker, "E. B. White: Notes and Comment by Author," *The New York Times*, July 11, 1969.

107 Paul Simon, "Father and Daughter," on *Surprise* (Sony Music, 2006).

108 Friedman, *Failure of Nerve*, 46.

109 Palmer, *Let Your Life Speak*, 10.

110 Marjorie J. Thompson lists all ten in her book *Soul Feast*. She cites William O. Paulsell, *Rules for Prayer* (New York: Paulist Press, 1993), and Martin Luther King Jr., *Why We Can't Wait* (New York: Signet Books, 1964), 3.

111 Flannery O'Connor, *Mystery and Manners: Occasional Prose* (New York: Farrar, Straus, and Giroux, 2000), 189.

112 Dietrich Bonhoeffer, *Life Together* (New York: HarperCollins, 1954), 27–28.

113 Andy Goldsworthy, *Rivers and Tides*, Directed by Thomas Riedelsheimer New Video Group, 2004. DVD.

114 Nouwen, "Moving From Solitude to Community," see n. 23.

115 From Pierre Ruhe, "Moving in the Spirit: Atlanta's Dance Safety Net for At-risk Youth," *Rhee Gold Company Blog*, November 1, 2009, http://www .dancestudiolife.com/2009/11/moving-in-the-spirit. To learn how to support this $550,000 program, visit www.movinginthespirit.org.

116 Ibid.

117 Ibid.

118 Cairns, *Love's Immensity*, 62.

119 Margaret J. Wheatley, *Leadership and the New Science: Discovering Order in a Chaotic World*, 3rd ed. (San Francisco: Berrett-Koehler, 2006), 40.

120 See Lesslie Newbigin, *The Gospel in a Pluralist Society* (Grand Rapids, MI: Wm. B. Eerdmans, 1989).

121 See Brian McLaren, *A Generous Orthodoxy* (Grand Rapids, MI: Zondervan, 2004) and *Everything Must Change: Jesus, Global Crises, and a Revolution of Hope* (Nashville: Thomas Nelson, 2007).

122 Edward Farley, *Faith and Beauty: A Theological Aesthetic* (Burlington, VT: Ashgate, 2001), 106.

123 This story of "Glas Gabhna" is retold by John O'Donohue in *Beauty: The Invisible Embrace* (New York: HarperCollins, 2004), 52.

124 This mapping technique has been refined by IDEO in *Design Thinking for Educators* (www.designthinkingforeducators.com).

125 Cairns, *Love's Immensity*, 99.

126 Wayne Muller, *Sabbath: Restoring the Sacred Rhythm of Rest* (New York: Bantam Books, 1999), 167, 168.

127 Rainer Maria Rilke, *Letters to a Young Poet* (New York: Random House, 1984), 24.

128 Ibid 24.

129 Samuel Sidney McClure, "Leonardo Da Vinci's Treatise on Painting" *The World's Greatest Books, v. 20*, (S. S. McClure Company, 1910), 233.

130 Quoted in Muller, *Sabbath*, 189, 190.

131 Mark Scandrette, *Practicing the Way of Jesus: Life Together in the Kingdom of Love* (Downers Grove, IL: InterVarsity Press, 2011), 188.

132 See Darrell L. Guder, *The Continuing Conversion of the Church* (Grand Rapids, MI: Wm. B. Eerdmans, 2000).

ABOUT PARACLETE PRESS

Who We Are

Paraclete Press is a publisher of books, recordings, and DVDs on Christian spirituality. Our publishing represents a full expression of Christian belief and practice—from Catholic to Evangelical, from Protestant to Orthodox.

We are the publishing arm of the Community of Jesus, an ecumenical monastic community in the Benedictine tradition. As such, we are uniquely positioned in the marketplace without connection to a large corporation and with informal relationships to many branches and denominations of faith.

What We Are Doing

Books Paraclete publishes books that show the richness and depth of what it means to be Christian. Although Benedictine spirituality is at the heart of all that we do, we publish books that reflect the Christian experience across many cultures, time periods, and houses of worship. We publish books that nourish the vibrant life of the church and its people—books about spiritual practice, formation, history, ideas, and customs.

We have several different series, including the best-selling Paraclete Essentials and Paraclete Giants series of classic texts in contemporary English; A Voice from the Monastery—men and women monastics writing about living a spiritual life today; award-winning poetry; best-selling gift books for children on the occasions of baptism and first communion; and the Active Prayer Series that brings creativity and liveliness to any life of prayer.

Recordings From Gregorian chant to contemporary American choral works, our music recordings celebrate sacred choral music through the centuries. Paraclete distributes the recordings of the internationally acclaimed choir Gloriæ Dei Cantores, praised for their "rapt and fathomless spiritual intensity" by *American Record Guide*, and the Gloriæ Dei Cantores Schola, which specializes in the study and performance of Gregorian chant. Paraclete is also the exclusive North American distributor of the recordings of the Monastic Choir of St. Peter's Abbey in Solesmes, France, long considered to be a leading authority on Gregorian chant.

Videos Our videos offer spiritual help, healing, and biblical guidance for life issues: grief and loss, marriage, forgiveness, anger management, facing death, and spiritual formation.

Learn more about us at our website: www.paracletepress.com, or call us toll-free at 1-800-451-5006.

SCAN TO READ MORE

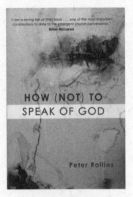

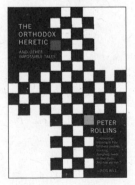